# DEDICATION

*To my parents, from whose example I learned
what faith is and how important it is to chase it.*

*To my wife, Tonya, for the love and support you give
me as we work to develop that faith in our children.*

First paperback edition 2020

Library of Congress Catalog Number: 2020917559
James, Josh
    Chasing the Storm: In Pursuit of a Faith That Works
    ISBN 978-1-7357296-0-2 (paperback)

Cross City Creations
Walnut, Mississippi 38683
www.crosscitycreations.com

# CHASING THE STORM

## IN PURSUIT OF A FAITH THAT WORKS

JOSH JAMES

**CROSS CITY CREATIONS**

# TABLE OF CONTENTS

# INTRODUCTION

## CONDITIONS ARE FAVORABLE

I REMEMBER THE FAINT FRAGRANCE OF FRESH-CUT trees and propane in the cool humidity. The blinding lights, flashing sparks, and roar of power tools still invade my eyes and ears. It's a combination of memories from a night I'll never forget. December 23, 2015, tornadoes tore through my hometown in Mississippi, turning a long stretch of it upside down. What was once thick forest was now a void. Only tree trunks and dirt remained; most of the trees were snapped in half and flat on the ground, while others were bent permanently into an eerie reminder of the storm's path of destruction.

My mind flashes forward a few months to the day I prepared my tax returns. "Were you impacted by a natural disaster during the year 2015?" Impacted—such a clinical, impersonal term. Did I endure "forcible contact" resulting in "a significant or major effect"? Guess what, Mr. Webster, I did. Along with dozens of neighboring families, my family faced several days of salvage, cleanup, and finding a new place to live.

The storm's impact, however, was not the strongest one we felt.

Because the touchdown occurred after sunset, we could not begin picking through the rubble until the next day. Morning came, and more than ten people (not including family, and only connected to us through our common faith) met us at the house to help salvage what remained of our belongings.

My family affectionately nicknamed the storm "The Grinch" because it tried to steal Christmas. We began cleanup on Christmas Eve morning. I can still see helpers dragging our artificial Christmas tree out the back door, frosted with dust and insulation. What about the boys' presents? We had a one-year-old and a six-week-old at the time, and we couldn't give them presents covered in fiberglass. On Christmas morning, however, my boys received so many donated gifts we could barely walk around my parents' living room without stepping on one. How? How did they do this? My heart grew three sizes that day.

Instead of being with their families, faithful people treated me and my family like theirs. On Christmas Day, one family we barely knew drove almost two hours, with their young children in the car, to bring us emotional and material support. A dear friend with no financial means "did what he could" by setting up a page for donations to help us with expenses. A Christian landlord offered a house for rent that he had been planning to advertise. We had moved into our area earlier in the year, and about twenty members of our former church drove two hours to help us unpack and settle into our new living arrangements.

A family from Jasper, AL, that had experienced the loss of their home in a 2011 tornado brought us a trailer full of household supplies. Malcolm, Julie, and Megan (via FaceTime) spent an hour sharing their story with us—how Christians had done the same for them when they were impacted by their storm. One of the funny things that has stuck in my memory was that we didn't have to buy toilet paper for several months afterward! Malcolm said he went more than a year without having to buy shaving cream because of the outpouring of faithful love shown by God's people.

Within a week, people acting on their faith took my upside-down world and set it upright again. That week I saw firsthand the power of nature, followed by the greater power of true Christian faith. The storm brought me fear; they brought encouragement. It brought me uncertainty; they brought direction. It stopped me in my tracks; they got me going again. Everything the tornado did to us was undone by people being faithful, kind, and compassionate. They did God's will on earth, becoming his feet and hands as they came to me in my despair and embraced me with his love.

Early Christians had a similar reputation, as expressed in Acts 17:6: "These who have turned the world upside down have come here too." We must understand the worldview was already flipped. These Christians were overturning a community that was upside down to begin with; they were setting it upright. How did they do it?

When my first child was about to be born, my friend Mario said, "Having a child will turn your whole world upside down, but then you will realize it's now the way it's supposed to be." True faith does the same thing.

Storm chasing began more recently than I expected—the earliest pioneer of the practice, David Hoadley, began chasing in 1956. Some do it for a hobby, but most chase tornadoes to observe them, learn how they form, and give warning to those in their paths as early as possible. We chase faith's storm in this book with a similar intent. We long to understand how to develop a faith that is more effective than nature—one that taps into the power of God and does his will on earth as it is done in heaven. At times, it will make us uncomfortable, like we are too close, but we must not stop until we take hold of it and put this upside-down world back on its feet. That's when we'll know we have a faith that works.

## DISCLAIMER

I am thankful to God there was no loss of life for my family—that storm did result in some casualties, including one in my community. While I was writing this book in 2020, a storm producing more damage and causing dozens of fatalities tore through the middle of Tennessee.

I do not intend with this book to minimize the grief and suffering these storms brought upon those families, and my heart aches for their losses. Whenever such loss happens, other people—even Christians—feel powerless against death. I realize we can offer only solace to those who are hurting. Even so, faith allows us to know we serve a God who will one day turn death itself upside down. Despite my powerlessness, I can rejoice.

Also, don't think I am glorifying destruction or saying it is acceptable for someone to be destructive in the name of Christianity. A destructive Christian is not embodying the virtues addressed in this book. Christian love rebuilds (1 Corinthians 8:1); those who destroy do not have God's love.

My intent is to reflect on the powerful way my life was impacted by the faith of others in the wake of the storm in 2015 and how their response offset the loss of property caused by the storm.

My family could easily have been in the house when the storm swept through. If I had to grieve the loss of them, perhaps I would not have considered myself restored by the faithful love of God's people in comparison. This crosses my mind almost daily—it has not escaped my attention.

I cannot get past the notion I was spared from grief because of God's mercy, and in light of the love and faith my family experienced, the loss of our property did not even remain a shadow.

## AN APOSTLE'S RECIPE FOR POWERFUL FAITH

Our Christian effectiveness has much in common with tornadoes.

For example, with relative confidence, we can know when a storm is developing with the capacity to produce tornadoes. We can measure the environment and recognize signs of a tornado's presence, like wind shear, variances in precipitation and lightning, and changes in temperature. During such a weather forecast, you might hear "conditions are favorable" to produce tornadoes.

This is the first idea Peter tackles in his second letter. "His divine power has given us everything relating to a godly life" (2 Peter 1:3). "Precious and great promises have been given to us so that through them you might become partners in the divine nature" (1:4). He is saying conditions are favorable for you to have a godly life that will make a significant impact!

Christians will produce change when their faith is properly supplemented. They will be effective. Look at the confidence Paul had in his influence on the early church. In Romans 1:13 he says, "Many times I have wanted to come to you so I could have some fruit with you also as I have with the rest of the nations." In Philippians 1:22 he says, "If I survive, the result is fruitful work for me." In his mind, being alive and around others was a guarantee of bearing fruit!

Unfortunately, for many of us, we are like the false teachers in Jude 12: "They are like waterless clouds pushed along by the wind." We offer the promise of rain and appear impressive, but despite favorable conditions and every advantage the gospel gives us, we end up being of little effect on our environment. Instead, we let our environment—the wind—determine where we go.

We are vocal about how our community and country should be but are silent when the time comes to make a difference. We are intent on confessing our love to Christ by sharing and liking posts on social media when "most people will just scroll by," but we disown him by our actions (Titus 1:16). We think we are taking part in the game of life, but like a deceptive older brother, Satan gives us the controller that's not plugged in. We feel like we are making a difference (like we're one of the big kids now), but we have no effect on those around us as we keep pushing buttons. We remain oblivious and irrelevant, but we are convinced we are contributing.

What does an unproductive faith look like? Picture a person who values getting involved in the work of the gospel, a person who has great intentions and wants to please God—yet, their faith is beset by frustration, disappointment, and an endless cycle that fails to improve. Unproductive faith manifests in congregations that become isolated from their communities or cannot get past petty disagreements. They "hold their own," but there is no fruit by which we would recognize them.

Let us remember when Jesus approached the fig tree in leaf, he did not praise the tree for its radiant foliage or strong roots. He cursed it for its lack of fruit. His repeated warning, "You will recognize them by their fruit," became a live demonstration. What happened to the beautiful leaves that still could have offered shade to a weary traveler, and what came of the strong trunk, which had been a figure in the community for many years? They withered.

A tree that does not produce fruit does not serve its purpose and is as profitable to Jesus as one that has already withered and died. In the same way, if a Christian yields no growth or fruit, no more is being accomplished by him or her than is being done now by those who have gone on before and are resting from their labors. The Christian who bears no fruit withers just as the fruitless tree. So does a congregation composed of such Christians!

For the Christian, productivity is less about getting finished than about getting results. How many of the teachings of Jesus emphasize the production of fruit? Matthew records statements in chapters 7, 12, 13, and 21. Mark does in chapters 4, 11, and 12. Luke does in chapters 6, 8, 13, and 20. John does in chapters 4 and 15, mentioning the concept seven times in chapter 15 alone.

For far too long Christians have focused only on being efficient and orderly (as Paul commands in I Corinthians 14:40), overlooking all the statements Jesus made about the requirement of fruit. We measure faithfulness in how many services the Christian attends. We measure congregational growth by how few disruptions occur—and whenever a disruption arises, we try to stifle it to keep the peace rather than examine it to see whether we have an opportunity to grow.

Unproductive churches pick a side of the fence, as though individual spiritual growth excludes the possibility of growth in numbers. We compromise one to gain the other and accuse congregations that grow in number of compromising the truth. We do this because we misunderstand true Christian productivity. When Peter says we should *supplement* our faith (1:5), the word does not denote an efficient system but a support system. It is *choreography*, not a *checklist*.

Much like the ligaments support the body (Ephesians 4:16, Colossians 2:19); much like the Spirit of Christ supported Paul in his imprisonment (Philippians 1:19); and much like God supports the sower by supplying seed (2 Corinthians 9:10), the "weather conditions" Peter teaches (2 Peter 1:5-7) will allow you to have a faith that not only acts but also impacts—his recipe for a powerful faith. When all the parts are out of sync, however, it falls apart.

In a theatrical production, the award is given not to the most efficient cast but to the cast whose parts work together the most effectively. Supplement your faith the way Peter tells us, and you will focus on your individual growth. At the same time, you will be encouraging others, exemplifying the gospel message of faith and love, and demonstrating integrity to a world thirsty for any kind of honesty.

Eventually, the impact you have on those around you will lead to growth in numbers, too. It is not "this one or the other," but "both or neither." Peter says, "If you have these qualities and are growing in them, they will keep you from being useless or unproductive in the knowledge of our Master" (1:8). "If you do these things, you will never fall" (1:10). "Entrance into the eternal kingdom of our Master and Savior, Jesus the Messiah, will be richly supplied to you" (1:11). Did you catch the wordplay in the final one? If *you* supply the virtues Peter extols, *God* will supply the entrance. Master these habits, and you will be productive and fruitful—and the result is the equivalent of a red carpet rolling out for you into God's eternal kingdom. If, however, you don't see the fruits, don't look forward to the day Jesus comes to inspect the tree.

## HOW TO GET THE MOST OUT OF THIS BOOK

In each chapter, we will study one of nine "weather conditions" an effective Christian displays. For each one, we will learn its importance, some examples of people who exhibited it, symptoms of a life without it, and how to recognize it in ourselves and others. Finally, we will explore a habit to practice for each condition so we can nurture it and make it flourish—so we can live EMPOWERED, an acronym we will use to remember them all.

We will describe this habit in two phases. The first will help you begin building it into your lifestyle. In most cases, this phase will have an inward focus, such as controlling your impulses or deepening your learning. The second phase of the habit will develop your skill even more and either turn the thoughts from Phase 1 into actions or channel your focus outward, using those habits to help others. Examples include controlling your responses and teaching someone what you have learned.

I recommend using a tracking system to help you keep up with these habits as you incorporate them into your lifestyle. Many options are available to you, and the most effective for you will depend on your preferences. An old-school approach would be to use a planner with a to-do list. Find a way to add each habit to your daily to-do list.

If your planner is not conducive to that or you don't want to change what has been working for you, the habit-tracking options on my website might be what you need. You can get a bookmark that provides space for you to track your habits. You can use the bookmark in your planner and have it at hand whenever you need it without messing with your planning flow. I also have a planning booklet available as a workbook or as a PDF.

If you are more technologically-minded, you can find dozens of habit tracking apps in both the Apple and Google app stores. I have used a handful of these, and which one works best will again depend on your preferences, but make sure it meets a few minimum requirements: It needs to let you add custom habits, not force you to pick from a predetermined selection, and it needs to be easy to use within your daily routine so you don't have to shut down your schedule to keep up with it.

Both Android and Apple have widget capabilities. These allow you to perform basic app functions without opening an app. I highly recommend you do this. For one reason, it does not disturb your workflow as much. For another, these widgets are easy to pull up accidentally, which serves as a reminder to keep on top of tracking your habits.

Finally, I like having access to my habit history so I can review reports of how many days in a row I have kept up a habit or what my longest streak is. This might not be a key motivator for you, but if it is, be sure your app will let you keep a tracking history.

What if you are stuck between the paper and digital planning worlds, or you like to write your notes by hand or draw on a planner but do not like carrying one with you? This is me, by the way—I have probably a half-dozen planners with the first three weeks filled in, and I have trouble throwing them away, so they just pile up! If this is you, what I do might work for you: I use my PDF planner in OneNote. OneNote allows you to create a page from a PDF and use a stylus or your finger to write in notes using all kinds of colors. It syncs to your other devices as well, so you can enter your notes on your computer and access them later with your phone or tablet. This lets me be paperless while writing notes by hand, which helps me remember what I wrote.

One of the key features of a good tracking system is the ability to measure your consistency over time. In my planner, I have set up one habit for each chapter. This way I can monitor all nine of them on one screen and determine whether I'm progressing toward my goals in each area. This also helps me hold myself accountable and make sure I work on all of the habits instead of cherry-picking the ones I think are easiest to maintain.

If you prefer your habit tracking to be a little more private, you can use the name of the characteristic you are trying to develop and not the vice you are trying to break. So if you do not want someone to know you are on a diet or trying to quit drinking, for example, enter "Overcome" as the habit name, and only you will know what weakness you are trying to overcome.

## TIPS FOR DEVELOPING THESE HABITS

The characteristics listed in 2 Peter 1:5-7 are not actions; they are the framework within which we take action. I cannot "do faith," but I act *based on* it. So I am not saying we need to automate them into mindless habits. On the contrary, the more you practice something, the better you can apply your focus and feelings to it. The habits are not the goal; they are the path to developing those characteristics.

For example, a musician would never confuse the piano scales she is practicing for music, but the better she becomes at ascending and descending from note to note, the better she will be at expressing herself in her songs. Changing notes becomes second nature, so her focus can be on the expression of the music. This ritual of practicing—though sometimes mindless and tedious—is necessary to allow her mind to focus on the feelings and emotions behind the notes. Her muscle memory is taking care of the notes and freeing her mind to access emotion. My show band director in college used to tell us, "You are playing the notes; I need you to play the music." In the case of Peter's characteristics, this should always be the goal. Do not practice these habits mindlessly—use the rigorous repetition to increase your ability, while you keep your mind and heart available to guide your actions like a compass.

**Be Systematic.** You might try to master both phases of each chapter's habit before moving onto the next one. Alternatively, you might master the first phase of each habit the first time you read the book and then come back to incorporate the second phase in a second read-through. In either case, do not pick and choose which habits or phases to practice. Each habit is a vital component of a productive faith. Your goal is to achieve balance, with each characteristic supplementing your character as evenly as possible. For example, you cannot be persistent without self-control, or love without being kind. Work on all of them, especially the ones you find most difficult.

**Let Them Synergize.** We have a video of my oldest son (when he was two years old) and his cousin performing a song in my parents' living room. His cousin was holding the microphone, and both of them were dancing while she sang. Whenever she held the microphone up to his face, he would stop moving, hunch over, and sing. He could not move and sing at the same time! As you learn a new habit, be sure not to abandon the ones you have already learned. It can be difficult to maintain them once you add others, but you must learn to sing and dance at the same time. The habits are supposed to work together like the instruments in an orchestra. Having one habit in abundance is like being at a concert where one of the instruments is too loud; the musician might be extremely talented, but if only one musician is audible, the song is ruined.

**Be Patient.** However you decide to work through the book, make sure you take the time to allow these habits to become second nature so you can develop the corresponding virtues. Do not rush the process. As you get a handle on a habit, it will become easier and require less focus—but at the beginning, you will be spending a lot of effort building the new habit and breaking its counterpart. As you work on diligence, you are fighting procrastination. As you work on self-control, you are susceptible to tunnel vision. Don't try to take on too many new habits at once, or it will be impossible to make a lasting change. Take your time and learn these habits the right way.

With time, you will begin to sense a change in your environment, like a cold front telling you something significant is about to happen. You will leave a profound impact on those around you, and it will be undeniable and unmistakable. The evidence will indicate a Christian has been spotted in your area, and the world will never be the same again. It is a long process, but you are not alone—together we will chase this storm, take hold of it, and come away empowered by a faith that works!

# CHASING THE STORM

## –PART I–

## STORM WARNING

# –I–

# DILIGENCE

## A COLD FRONT IS COMING IN

*"Men regret the sorrow which they feel for worldly losses, but
they do not regret the sorrow which cures sin."*
—*Plummer, II Corinthians, 222.*

FOR HUNDREDS OF YEARS, ISRAEL WAVERED BETWEEN worshiping the God of Israel and the gods of the nations around them. In response to Ahab's imposed worship of Baal and other Canaanite deities, Elijah asked the people in 1 Kings 18:21, "How long will you waver between two choices? If the Lord is God, follow him—if Baal is, follow him!" But the people did not respond.

Thematically, you can link this back to Joshua 24:15, when Joshua told the Israelites, "Decide today whom you will serve." Although those present in Joshua's day were adamant they would follow God, now hundreds of years have passed, and many are stuck between two options. They cannot bring themselves to commit to a decision.

Elijah set out to change that. On Mount Carmel he challenged the prophets of Baal to a showdown to determine the truth. When the God of Israel responded in the challenge by consuming his sacrifice, the people decided: "The Lord! He is God!" (18:39). But as in the days of Joshua, their decision was short-lived.

The church at Corinth also struggled with commitment to God. The issues plaguing that congregation would make many modern Christians blush. The

Corinthians defended their rights and flaunted their gifts without considering what was best for one another, driving weak Christians back to idolatry. Some were going to court against one another. Others argued with one another about who had the best spiritual mentor (Paul, Apollos, Cephas). They trash-talked Paul to the point that he had to address them in 2 Corinthians 10:1: "I who am 'humble when face-to-face with you, but brash toward you when absent.'" One of the Corinthian Christians married his own father's wife—and the congregation did not seem bothered by these problems.

Like a loving father doling out discipline, Paul wrote to them in terms many parents have echoed, which "hurt him as much as them." He even says he regretted sending the letter for a while: "Although I upset you with that letter, I do not regret it—although I did" (2 Corinthians 7:8). What made him feel differently?

He goes on to say, "I am aware of how my letter brought you to grief for a time since it was necessary, but now I rejoice—not because you were brought to grief, but because you were brought to a kind of grief that produced repentance." He continues, "Godly grief accomplishes repentance that leads to salvation, which is not to be regretted. But worldly grief brings about death. Look how this very same experience of godly grief produced so much diligence in you" (2 Corinthians 7:10-11). Yes, he goes on to talk about the other things grief produced in them, but first it brought them diligence. Like Israel nine centuries earlier, the winds of change arrived, and the full attention of the congregation was on the decision they could no longer avoid. "I must be better than this."

For sports fans, 1994 proved to be a crazy year. I grew up watching baseball, and that year the season was shortened because of a strike by the players' union. Michael Jordan, who retired from the NBA in 1993, played baseball for the Birmingham Barons, a minor-league affiliate of the Chicago White Sox. The San Francisco 49ers won 13 games on their way to their first Super Bowl without Joe Montana. O.J. Simpson led the LAPD on the most televised police chase in history.

The most unbelievable athletic accomplishment from that year was when fourteen-year-old Venus Williams made her professional debut as a tennis player. She won her first match, in straight sets, against a woman ranked #57 in the world. She advanced to play the top-ranked woman in the world and won the first set and three games of the second, but she ended up losing the match. Sponsors such as Reebok and Nike courted her, and every news channel talked about her—not just sports channels. Where did this young phenom come from, and what will she do by the time she's full-grown?

Then in 1997 her sister Serena, younger than Venus by one year, shocked the world by beating the player ranked #4 in the world, Monica Seles. The Williams sisters went on to win a combined thirty grand slam events over the next two decades. What are the chances a pair of siblings would reach this level of success?

Most people don't realize the story began far earlier than 1994. The girls' father, in an attempt to have them discovered by tennis scouts, recorded them playing tennis against each other at the age of seven (Serena) and eight (Venus) years old. They had other siblings, too: three sisters who practiced but did not have the success Venus and Serena did. One of them, Isha, told the New York Times in 2012, "Life was get up, 6 o'clock in the morning, go to the tennis court, before school. After school, go to tennis. But it was consistency. I hate to put it [like this], but it's like training an animal. You can't just be sometimey with it."

As Joshua told Israel, "Decide today." The Williams sisters made their mark on the tennis world in the 1990s, but their work started a decade earlier on courts where no one was watching, while everyone else their age slept or played. The Williams family decided they were going to be great, and they began the habit of working toward greatness.

## WEATHER REPORT

The day the tornado came through my community in 2015, the high was 73 degrees Fahrenheit—in December! The low overnight was 51 degrees. What brought that storm (and what brings all tornadoes) to fruition was a combination of two things: a strong cold front and a warm updraft of air. If the cold front sweeps in at a high altitude, it begins to sink as the hotter air below rises. If the front continues feeding cold air at that altitude, the hot and cold will begin rolling over each other. Then, if the right updraft of warm air happens, the cloud tips over, starting a mesocyclone (like a tornado, but high in the atmosphere).

The swirling in the sky has the same effect as stirring a drink—the spiral goes all the way to the bottom, and anything at the bottom gets pulled upward. Yes, the funnel cloud gets all the credit, but it is an extension of the mesocyclone, and the mesocyclone only exists because of the presence of both a strong cold front and a warm updraft of air.

Diligence is the cold front. You can sense it in the environment. It is determined, focused, and directed like wind.

More than ten times in the New Testament, we are warned to be diligent. "Be diligent to present yourself to God" (2 Timothy 2:15); "Be diligent to keep the unity of the Spirit" (Ephesians 4:3); "Be diligent to make your calling and election sure" (2 Peter 1:10). What do they have in common? There is always a purpose—an aim—of diligence. In many of these examples, this is the "to do" part of the instruction. The goal might be long term, like entering God's sabbath rest (Hebrews 4:11), or a personal plan, like visiting Paul before winter (2 Timothy 4:21).

Whatever the circumstance, diligence involves two things: planning and priority. It decides what must be done and what must be done now to obtain the desired result. If you have one or the other, you will likely accomplish nothing. You might have urgency but no plan, which yields poor results, or you might have a plan but no urgency, in which case you never make progress.

At one time in Greek literature, the word Peter uses here, the word we translate as diligence, referred to speed—how quickly someone did something. This might be in view in a few passages from the New Testament. One is Mark 6:25, where Herod's daughter, after Herod told her to ask him for anything, consulted with her mother and "immediately went in to the king *in haste*." The other is Luke 1:39, where Mary "went to the hill country *in haste*" after learning Elizabeth was with child. But even in these passages, there might be something more. One author suggests the phrasing "reflects the innermost condition of a perturbed, thinking mind." That is, the physical speed with which they went is not the point; instead, the issue is the urgency or anxiety of mind that drove them to act in the first place.[1]

---

[1]Hospodar, B. (1956). "META SPOUDES" IN LK 1,39. The Catholic Biblical Quarterly, 18(1), 16.

Other words based on the same root occur in the form of adverbs, adjectives, and verbs. As an adverb, it is used to describe how the Jews urged Jesus *earnestly* to heal the centurion's servant (Luke 7:4). As an adjective, it is used to describe how Titus felt about helping the churches gather monetary aid for churches in need (2 Corinthians 8:17). Paul used the verb form many times to emphasize actions his readers should do: "*Be diligent* to present yourself to God acceptably" (2 Timothy 2:15); "*Be diligent* to preserve the Spirit's unity in the bond of peace" (Ephesians 4:3). Each case requires urgency, dedication, care, and priority. Those who are leaders in the church must attend to this, as Paul directs: "Whoever leads must do so *diligently*," and "*diligently* prevent yourself from being lazy" (Romans 12:8,11).

So why do many of us struggle to be diligent? What causes us not to care? What keeps us from responding with urgency about things that are important to us?

In some cases it is mere procrastination; in others, it is distraction. Jesus talked about some of these people who struggle with these obstacles when he said, "These are the ones who hear the Word, but their anxieties for this age, the deception of wealth, and their desires for other things come in and choke the Message, so it becomes unproductive" (Mark 4:19). These are three different thorns that share a common thread and produce the same result: fruitlessness.

## ANXIETY FOR THIS AGE

> *"Do not love the world or what is in the world, because*
> *whoever loves the world does not have God's love in him.*
> *Everything in the world—the desire of the body, the desire*
> *of the eyes, and the arrogance of life—is not from the Father*
> *but is of the world. And the world is passing away along*
> *with its desires, but whoever does God's will lives forever."*
> —I John 2:15-17

Anxiety can be a funny thing. In Matthew 14, Jesus spent the night in prayer after feeding five thousand people and teaching them for a significant part of the day. As he began his time of solitude, his disciples boarded a boat and began to sail across the Sea of Galilee. During the early morning hours, he came toward them walking on the water.

They are terrified, thinking he is a ghost. Peter, in a move that proves he knew who Jesus was, says, "If it is you, tell me to come to you on the water." Think about it. If you doubted the person walking toward you on the sea was Jesus, why would you trust them to tell you to step out of the boat? He must have known this was Jesus, so despite the fears of some of those around him, he does the impossible—he walks on water.

What happens next? He begins to take note of the strong wind, becomes afraid, and sinks into the water. In his mind, would he not reason that if Jesus can make the sea support Peter's feet, he also can keep him safe despite the weather? But that's the thing with worry—it is not reasonable. It convinces you that you missed something, despite facts and evidence to the contrary.

Several New Testament authors addressed this problem. Matthew 6:25-34 uses multiple illustrations and encouragements to warn us not to let worry control us: "Do not be anxious about your life—what you will eat or what you will drink or for your body, what you will wear. Is life not more than food, and the body more than clothing?" Let's remember the context. Verse 25 begins with "Because of this." This means we need to look back at verse 24 to pinpoint why Jesus was addressing the anxiety of life: "No one can serve two masters. He will either hate one and love the other, or he will become attached to one and neglect the other. You cannot serve both God and money." This statement is the impetus for those final ten verses of the chapter! This is also supported by verse 33: "Seek God's kingdom and righteousness first." To be anxious about this world is to attach yourself to something other than God. Peter's attention in that instant attached to the wind and waves; thus he neglected the safety he had with Christ.

We risk losing our safety when we place too much emphasis on this present world. Whether we're distracted by suffering in the present age (Romans 8:18) or the indulgent behaviors this world takes for granted (I Peter 4:1-6), we must remember they are temporary and are not worth our future!

No time is more crucial for you than right now. You will either do what you dreamed of yesterday or what you will regret tomorrow. When you look back on today, either it will be part of your path to success or part of the detour where you got lost. It will be the day you had enough trust to leave the boat or the day you lost trust and began to sink.

Don't be overwhelmed. Peter learned firsthand what it meant to fall short of the Lord's expectations while trying to become a leader. After he went so far as to deny Jesus three times on the night Jesus was betrayed, I wonder if he thought it was over. Jesus was dead, Peter had been afraid to tell a servant girl he was a follower of Jesus, and no one knew what to do next—but that's not the end of the story. Jesus was raised! He appeared to the disciples on several occasions, and during one of those appearances, he asked Peter a simple, soul-searching question: "Do you love me more than these?"

As Peter turned his attention to the fish sizzling over the fire in the morning light, and then back to the Author of his salvation, he had a decision to make.

He doesn't cower again. He boldly proclaims the resurrection of Jesus in Jerusalem, despite multiple arrests and physical punishment. In the process, he learns a valuable lesson about God's patience: Although he made mistakes and fell short of expectations, he could make everything right—but it would take full-on, no-holds-barred dedication from there on out.

He would go on to write, "Since you know this [current world] will be dissolved, what kind of people should you be with holy conduct and devotion? ... So, dear friends, as you await these things, be diligent to be found unstained and blameless by him in peace, and consider our Master's patience to mean salvation." Jesus had been patient with him as he failed to walk on water, as he drew his sword in the garden to fight a mob just before denying him in front of a servant girl, and as he went back to the only life he knew after Jesus' death—and he saved Peter from the waves, the angry mob, and the prison of self-defeat.

## A DESIRE FOR OTHER THINGS

*"The number one priority is playing baseball. There are so many people in New York trying to get you to do this and get you to do that, which is fine, but you have to take care of yourself."*
—Derek Jeter

The human body has a way of telling you exactly what it wants. If it wants something badly enough, it drowns out everything else to arrest your attention. Of course, this is a survival trait—if we didn't have loud reminders when we are hungry or tired, we wouldn't take proper care of ourselves.

But sometimes what the body wants is not what it needs. This might be the case when your body craves a second piece of cake or wants to punch someone in the face while they are arguing with you. So you end up having to tell your body to stand down—like you would a toddler. "You cannot have that right now, and I don't care if you don't like me. A good body does not act like this. A good body behaves."

These inclinations toward impulsive, self-destructive actions make no sense to outside observers because they're not reasonable. They are fueled by desire masquerading as necessity. With childlike dishonesty, desire allows you to see only what will make you gratify it. We must be diligent to examine all the details and verify what we believe is actually true.

That is what the Berean Christians were commended for doing in Acts 17:11. They welcomed the message eagerly and spent every day examining the Scriptures to verify those things were right. The old tradition was not their master—the Scripture was. When the potential for conflict arose, Scripture won every time, and any conflicting tradition was discarded.

1 John 2:15 applies here, too. The desires of this body and the desires of our eyes are going to pass away with this world. They are temporary. Of course, this doesn't mean they aren't enticing! Refer to the book of Genesis and you will recognize this playing out from the very first sin committed by humankind. When Eve was tempted, she saw the fruit was "good for food" (something her body would like to eat), it was a "delight to the eyes," and it was attractive because it would "make her wise" (Genesis 3:6)—all three of John's forms of loving the world! When she had to choose between this one meal and immortality in the garden, she gave up eternity immediately.

The same is said of Esau in chapter 25. Jacob had been cooking while Esau was out in the field. He came in exhausted and hungry and sold his birthright to Jacob for one meal. He said, "I am about to die; what good is a birthright to me?" The chapter ends with the statement, "So Esau despised his birthright."

Now, this gives us a little clue into what Jesus meant about the impossibility

wizardry do they use to discern which strategy will win? How are they ahead of their opponents' game plan?

They aren't. A fair amount of their action is in *response* to the opponents' plan. A good coach's preparation and quick action will mask much of that guesswork. This is because they see the potential choices facing their opponent. They do the research. They examine their opponents' options and choose which is the most likely action. Finally, they put their best effort toward stopping that, leaving some margin in case they guess incorrectly. This whole process is their plan.

If I don't understand how to do that, it looks like that good coach is faster, stronger, or a cheater. It is like magic because if I were the coach, my outcome would have been much worse. So what do I do? I make excuses. I say the deck is stacked against me and I lack the time or resources to succeed. Despite the importance of the task ahead, I complain about my helplessness. But I must remember 2 Peter 1:3: "His divine power has given us everything that relates to godly life." I have the resources, and I have as much time as everyone else; the only difference is where and how I spend it. What I do not have is an excuse. As C. S. Lewis put it, "It might be hard for an egg to turn into a bird; it would be a jolly sight harder for it to learn to fly while remaining an egg."

Through Christ, God gave us everything we need to make it—everything we need to let us share in His divine nature. That does not mean it's easy to put on diligence (or the qualities we have yet to examine in the coming chapters). But it is "a jolly sight harder" for us to be productive in our faith without applying diligence. This is why diligence is first in the list of qualities. This is why we must be diligent to supplement our faith with each of the other qualities. Peter assumes diligence and faith will be present from the beginning. Without these two, none of the others are possible.

## PHASE 1: MAKE A PLAN

Much has been written about the art and science of planning, but the method you use is a lot like starting a diet—consistency is key. Someone who consistently uses a mediocre planning system will fare better than someone who occasionally flirts with a great one. Try different systems to discover what works for you, but when you find it, KEEP USING IT.

**Stay consistent.** If you use a daily system, use it daily. If weekly, use it weekly. Planning only half the time will result in twice the stress because your mind will not trust you to follow through. Anxiety about missing something will plague you. If you consistently use your system, you will watch those little worries go away as your mind trusts you to remember at the right time and lets you off the hook. Consistency is a vital part of solidifying each habit in this book. Without it, you destroy any long-term impact your faith can have.

**Stay simple.** My system is simple. I started with my lifelong goals and created milestones to get me there. I broke those milestones down into monthly steps and made weekly goals based on them. Don't overthink planning—it is much more important *that* you do it than *how* you do it. If your system is too elaborate to remember or fit into a busy lifestyle, you will be inconsistent too often for it to make a difference. If you want assistance with determining your goals and breaking them down into a workable plan, use the system I provide in the section titled "Aftermath."

**Stay realistic.** An impossible plan will result in stress and failure. It does you no good to plan to lose seventy-five pounds in two months or become fluent in Japanese in six weeks—but we can meet realistic milestones even before the deadline. Strive for those. Research what health professionals say is a healthy number of pounds to lose per week and go from there. Download a language learning app and try to do a lesson every day. Although you did not reach the impossible goal you originally wanted, you have made a great start and can visualize yourself increasing in skill as time goes on.

## Phase 2: Make Progress

Although we might consider these two phases one habit, they involve distinct skills. The first skill is how to schedule your time, allot your resources, and decide on a destination. The second is STICKING TO THE PLAN. It is one thing to put together a budget for your family but another to live within that budget. It is one thing to begin a diet but another to live within its requirements. So after you form the habit of creating a plan, more work awaits if you want to *do* what you planned. This is Phase 2.

**Grasp the gravity of the situation now.** Diligence has a way of teaching you through your failures as much as through your successes. For example, if your diet needs work, you might begin with good intentions but not follow through. Eventually, you reach a point where a change must be made—blood pressure issues, heart disease, etc. Somehow it becomes easier to make changes because we sense what will happen imminently if we do not change. At that point, though, you have endangered yourself! How much better would it be for you to see where you *will* be with the same urgency you would feel if you already had a serious diagnosis? Not only are you nowhere near the same physical danger, but also many more options are available to you, such as being able to build yourself up to a better quality of life. Which of the two options gives you the greatest likelihood of getting to spend more quality time with your family? Learn to sense the urgency in advance, and you will not reach the point of crisis!

**Remove your big rocks first.** Some people "want to do better about" something, but that desire doesn't take precedence over the decisions they make every day. We touched on Jesus' parable of the sower, in which he said people become unproductive when they allow certain thorns to choke out the Word. Earlier in that parable, Jesus talks about a type of heart he calls "rocky soil." This type of heart receives the Message, recognizes its urgency, and makes a plan, but because certain rocks were not removed first, it is short-lived. Sticking to a plan often requires you to say *no* to some strong habits—big rocks. It can seem like it isn't worth the effort to remove them now, so you decide to do it later—but how can you expect to remove the rocks *after* you finish planting? You will destroy the crop then. The rocks must go now. For me, an example of a time when this worked was a summer when I suffered severe anxiety. As an escape, I spent too much time on social media. The big rock I needed to remove required me to buy a flip phone (the cheapest, lowest-featured device I could find) and use that for six weeks. When I finally went back to my smartphone, I was strong enough to avoid those social media apps. From time to time now, I will delete the apps and only access social media through my phone's web browser. The inconvenience of not using the app means I spend less time on my phone and more on my goals.

**Take one milestone at a time.** When you run a long-distance race, such as a half-marathon, you must worry about more than physical deficiencies like low blood sugar, low stamina, or dehydration. A difficult hurdle for many runners is the mental determination to finish. One piece of advice given to long-distance runners is to "chase one jersey at a time." Because the race is long, you cannot afford to run headlong past everyone at the beginning—but you trained and worked for this very moment, so you will catch them eventually. As you pass other competitors one by one, spend a little time mentally celebrating a small victory. Thus, you take a single long-distance event and reduce it to many games consisting of a few hundred yards each. You can do the same thing with the goals you set in Phase 1. If your goal is a diet, for example, celebrate every three to five pounds you lose. If your plan is financial health, celebrate every week you stay within your budget. Do not, however, let your celebration knock you out of the habit! The purpose of celebrating small milestones is to keep you *in* the habit. So if you eat at an expensive restaurant to celebrate staying within your budget for the week, you have undone the work that got you there!

This first habit—doing what you plan to do—is essential to your success with the rest of the goals in this book. It is the cold front that brings on the storm—the driving force that leads you to turn your world upside down. Learn diligence and how to apply it, and the winds of change will come. The skies are growing dark as a powerful faith approaches.

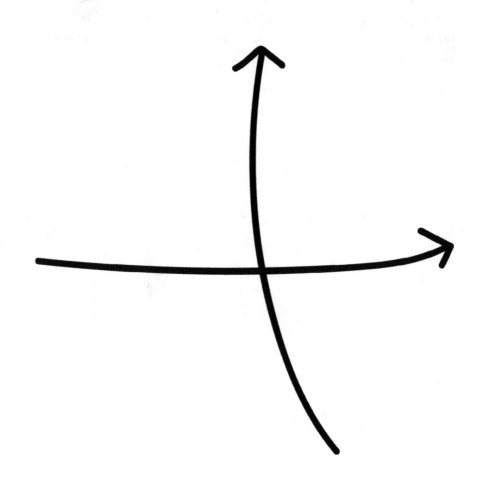

# –II–

# FAITH

## A WARM UPDRAFT OF AIR
## AT THE RIGHT TIME

*"Efforts and courage are not enough
without purpose and direction."*
—*John F. Kennedy*

EARLY IN THE MORNING, THE SUN BEGINS TO PEEK over the hills. A few quiet moments pass while the old man packs a bag and saddles it to his donkey. He calls two of his men to travel with him and his son. The journey will take a few days as they traverse the wilderness—hill country—so the task ahead is not an easy one.

On the third day, the old man raises his weary eyes, and his heart sinks—today is the day. He stops and turns toward his companions. "Stay here with the donkey. The boy and I will go worship, and we'll be back later."

As they make their way closer, his son checks again to ensure they have brought everything they need. There is the wood and the flint, and there is the rope for tying the animal to the altar. The animal! Where is the lamb for the sacrifice? Dad must have forgotten it! "Father, we have the supplies for the fire and the wood for the altar, but where is the animal for our sacrifice?"

"The Lord will provide, my son."

I wonder if Abraham kept looking up at that fateful mountain as he turned from his companions to go where God had directed him. Did he have second thoughts? Was he fully resolute in his decision to obey what God had commanded him to do?

The text of Genesis 22:1-8 only tells us about Abraham's behavior—what he did and said. All we know is he was willing to journey through the wilderness, tie up his son, lay him on the altar, and raise his knife to kill him. Did he think his situation was unfair? Did he question God's plan? After all, God was the one who told him, "All the world will be blessed through Isaac."

In Hebrews 11 we find the answer. "By faith, when Abraham was tested, he sacrificed Isaac, and the one who received the promises offered up his only son. To him the promise was given, 'Your lineage will be called in Isaac.' He figured God was able to raise him from the dead—from where he did receive him back, figuratively speaking."

Why is that significant? By the time we read the chapters leading to Genesis 22, we see nothing about God raising anyone from the dead. How did Abraham reach that conclusion? How could he figure that God would raise Isaac from the dead? Well, God had promised him Isaac would carry the lineage of Abraham. So if Abraham killed Isaac at God's request, to keep his promise, God would *have* to raise him from the dead!

In the book of Habakkuk, we travel with the prophet on a journey from what I like to call *if* faith to *though* faith. As his prophecy begins, the situation is not optimistic. Nebuchadnezzar and his army have conquered many of the nations surrounding Judah. A century earlier, Assyria conquered the northern kingdom of Israel. God's people were at the brink of genocide. Habakkuk begins his complaint: "O Lord, how long must I cry out for help and you not listen? I shout 'Violence!' to you and you do not save!" (Habakkuk 1:2). If we put this into the terms we would use today, "God, why do you let bad things happen to good people despite their obedience to you?"

Habakkuk does not receive a favorable response. God tells him not only is he aware of what is happening, but he is also behind it. God himself is raising the "bitter and hasty nation" of Nebuchadnezzar to its seat of power! Wait a minute—how is that fair? How could the God of Israel be fighting against them for the other guys? In Habakkuk's phrasing, "Why do you stay quiet when the wicked consumes the one more righteous than he?" (1:13). Feeling confident God is the one in the wrong here, Habakkuk stands at his watch post and waits for a response to his complaint—the ultimate "I need to speak to the manager" moment.

God's answer this time (2:2-20) lets Habakkuk know he's been looking at this the wrong way. "Write the vision." In other words, what God told Habakkuk will happen for certain—the conquest of Judah by Babylon. And even if there is a fleeting hope they will escape the clutches of Nebuchadnezzar, they will not. But Nebuchadnezzar will be judged, too.

"Look—his soul is arrogant and does not do what is right, but the righteous one will live by his faith." He proceeds to detail how Nebuchadnezzar will be judged for hoarding treasures he stole from other nations and building his city on blood, all while touting the strength of his false gods. God will silence it all in time.

Read Habakkuk 2. How many statements are directed toward Habakkuk's primary concern—the people of Judah? How much time does God spend advising them on how to escape? Perhaps two statements could be directed toward them. The second we will address first: "The Lord is in his holy temple; let all the earth keep silent before him."

When Nebuchadnezzar worshiped his idols, he set them up and commanded the metal or wooden objects to act on his behalf. "Woe to him who tells a wooden thing to wake up or a speechless stone to get up. Can this thing teach? Look—it is overlaid with gold and silver, but there is no breath in it" (2:19). God addressed two major problems with idol worship—the image's creator worships the created image, and the created image has no power! No, the Lord is our Creator, and he is in his holy temple. No one can come into his temple and tell him to wake up or get up. They must remain silent before him because he is the master and teacher; they are the servants and students.

The other statement is "The righteous one will live by his faith." This is a key statement from Habakkuk because the New Testament authors quote him three times. Paul uses the phrase twice, in Romans 1:17 and Galatians 3:11, and the author of Hebrews quotes it once, in Hebrews 10:38. None of these have Nebuchadnezzar in view; all three passages beg us to be faithful to Christ despite the difficulties and persecutions we will meet.

In Romans, Paul is talking about how God will judge those who suppress the truth with their disobedience, but the righteous will live by faith. In Galatians, he is combating those who say observing the tenets of the Mosaic Law brings righteousness. Instead, righteousness was based on faith because "whoever is under the Law is under a curse." In Hebrews, the author addresses willful disobedience before quoting this passage. "We do not belong to the group who retreats and is destroyed but rather to the one who has faith to preserve the soul." Faith is how it's done!

In the end, Habakkuk refers to the revelation from God about what was about to happen: "I take it in, and my body trembles; my lips quiver at the sound." "Yet I will quietly wait for the disastrous day to come upon those who attack us."

How could he put aside all the noise of "bad things happening to good people" he had wondered about earlier?

The very first word in Habakkuk 3:17 shows us something has changed with his perspective. Earlier, his faith depended on what he thought was right, almost like, "If this is what will happen, why does God deserve our worship?" He had *if* faith. Now he resolves, "Though the fig tree may not blossom, yet I will rejoice in the Lord. I will find joy in the God of my salvation." He possesses *though* faith. That's a faith one could live by! Perhaps Abraham also thought, "Though God told me to kill my son, I can do it because God will not break his promise to bless the world through Isaac."

## WEATHER REPORT

*"Faith is taking the first step*
*even when you don't see the whole staircase."*
—Martin Luther King, Jr.

If diligence is the cold front, faith is the updraft of warm air that gets the storm going. Faith gives an upward direction—a purpose—to everything we do.

Many people like to comfort someone with the phrase, "Everything happens for a reason." I don't agree with this sentiment. Sometimes bad things happen, or we struggle, and it's just meaningless. We see news reports of mindless violence or children abused by those they trusted. Can we say there is an acceptable reason these atrocities happened? Aren't we unfair when we say,

"This is what God must want"? What could someone need to learn so badly that such tragedies could be justified?

If I may, let me offer a different thought: "Everything that happens has a purpose." At first glance, this might not appear to be much of a difference—but the perspective makes the difference! Since something bad already happened, I have the chance to respond as Jesus would. When I react to losses in life by focusing on God's glory, my mind drifts upward to the throne of God. My focus rises to "think about the things above, where Christ is seated at the right hand of God" (Colossians 3:1). Faith is a warm updraft, driven that direction by a diligent cold front. When these two qualities work in tandem, the same result will follow every time.

Peter knew this firsthand and made purpose a theme of his message. Consider his sermon in Acts 2:36: "So all the house of Israel must know for certain, God has made this Jesus—whom you crucified—both Master and Messiah." Why did the people reject God's message to the point they killed his dear Son? What acceptable excuse could they offer?

He doesn't elaborate on the reasons why. Instead, he shows how God took their violence and insolence and used them for his purpose. When the people give their distress signal—"What can we do?"—Peter gives them purpose: "Repent! Each of you must be baptized in the name of Jesus Christ for the forgiveness of your sins, and you will receive the gift of the Holy Spirit." In Acts 3:19 he tells them, "Repent and change, so your sins can be wiped out!" In effect, "What's done is done, but despite that, you can be saved and bring future meaning to meaningless sin."

Alcoholics Anonymous picked up on this concept as well. The organization's Twelve Promises include, "We will not regret the past nor wish to shut the door on it." The most hideous, hurtful past can be used powerfully by the Christian in recovery.

Paul himself acknowledges, "I give thanks to the one who empowered me—Christ Jesus our Lord—because he considered me faithful and gave me a ministry, even though I was once a blasphemer, persecutor, and violent person. But I received mercy because I did these things unknowingly because of a lack of faith." Paul never tried to shut the door on his past life. Instead, he shouted, "If Jesus can save me, he'll save you too!"

## FAITH DOES NOT SAY WHY BAD THINGS HAPPEN; IT TELLS THE WORLD WHY WE ENDURE THEM.

For Peter, this happens again in Acts 5:41 after he and John are arrested by the Sanhedrin, interrogated, and threatened not to speak of Jesus. "So they went out of the presence of the Sanhedrin celebrating because they were considered worthy to suffer dishonor because of the Name."

Search for the reason Peter and John had to endure this suffering, and you will find that those religious leaders were self-seeking and sought to protect their interests. They refused to accept the evidence of the resurrection exhibited by the apostles in the miracles they performed. Because of that arrogant stubbornness, they killed Jesus, mistreated Peter and John, and made many people in the city afraid to commit to this new Way.

Trying to find the reason for such suffering likely would lead many of us to become embittered and blame God. Peter and John endured the suffering, and instead of asking why, they found a purpose for it—taking part in Jesus' suffering. Let's not forget, this is the same Peter who wrote those two short letters placed near the end of the New Testament. With this in mind, some of his statements resonate with much more power.

"You rejoice in him, even though for a little while—if need be—you have been hurt by various trials so the testing of your faith (which is more valuable than gold that perishes even though it has been tried by fire) might be discovered to result in praise, glory, and honor at the appearance of Jesus Christ" (I Peter 1:6-7). In the next two verses, he talks about how his readers love Jesus even though they have never met him. They are faithful to him even though they do not see him. So they can rejoice with inexpressible joy at the salvation of their souls, which he goes on to call "the goal of your faith." The purpose of our faith, the finish line, is our final salvation at the return of Jesus. Everything we endure in this life is endured with that end in mind.

Peter also uses the unfair mistreatment of Jesus to exemplify finding purpose when we suffer unfairly. "You were called for this purpose—because Christ died for you to leave a template behind for you so you could follow in his footsteps. He did not sin and no deceit was found in his mouth. Though verbally abused, he did not abuse in return. Though he suffered, he did not threaten. Instead, he

Priests under the Law of Moses were required to offer a sacrifice for their own sins before offering one for the sins of the people. Like them, the father in Mark 9:22 first needed to ask for a "cure" for himself before asking the Lord to intervene for someone else. Some evidence of faith was present but not enough. A supplement was needed.

Imagine a friend of yours comes to you worried. "I have been so tired the past few weeks; I can barely make it through the day. My knuckles are like sandpaper, and the slightest inconvenience sets me off into a tantrum. Am I losing my mind?" At your advice, she schedules an appointment with her doctor and calls you about it that evening. "The doctor said my thyroid is the problem. Blood tests confirmed I need to take medicine every day to correct it." Within a week, she comes by for a visit, and the fire is back in her eyes—instead of in her temper. Life is good now that balance has returned.

The apostle gives us a similar prescription in 2 Peter 1:5: "Supplement your faith." Recognize the wording—in Peter's list of qualities, faith is assumed. Nowhere in his letter does he direct them to "supply [something] with faith." Faith must be present from the start.

Peter is using an ancient Greek literary device called a *sorites*, where each item in the list produces or is the basis for the next. Despite the strange vocabulary, the *sorites* is a concept a child can understand. "There Was an Old Lady Who Swallowed a Fly" is a more recent example! The fly led to the spider, the spider to the bird, and so on until she swallowed a horse and "died, of course."

Faith is first in the list, so it must exist before the other items can. Since love is the final item, it is the ultimate goal of faith and cannot be attained unless each characteristic listed between them is present in abundance. To return to the story of the old lady who swallowed a fly—if she had stopped after the spider, she would likely have been fine. The chain of causes and effects stops wherever the cycle breaks.

This is the secret to a faith that works! The mistake we make is to treat these characteristics like a potluck meal.

Let's say kindness and virtue resonate with me, but I struggle with self-control. I might be tempted to take a larger portion of the qualities that make me feel better about myself and treat the difficult ones like mystery meat. In a *sorites*, however, you cannot achieve the last item—the most important one—without all the ones leading up to it. Each of these qualities is of equal importance, and we must hone them to near perfection before we will reap the benefits promised in verses 8-11.

I have seen signs posted in fellowship halls and church buildings that state, "No Food Beyond This Point." Potluck is intended to take place only in its designated area. If you have a sign like this where you worship, may it also remind you there is no place for a potluck approach to developing Christian habits!

Faith is the starting point for everything else in the Christian's life. "Whatever does not come from faith is sin" (Romans 14:23). On this cornerstone, all the Christian habits rest. Without it, they fall at the first sign of adversity. Conversely, faith without any of these other qualities is anemic and starving. It only works if we supply it with the spiritual nutrients it needs.

Thus, developing faith is much broader than one habit can address. But each of the facets of faith and faithfulness will be addressed as we come to each chapter. Faith is the foundation for virtue, knowledge, control, persistence, and so on. Our habit for this chapter will be to develop and maintain an upward focus through worship.

## STARTING TO LIVE EMPO**W**RED (WORSHIP)

*"Faith is not the belief that God will do what you want. It is the belief that God will do what is right."*
—*Max Lucado*

Psychologists sometimes refer to the H.A.L.T. method when working with people who are fighting addiction. Its principle applies also to those who fall into bad habits of all kinds. When a person is tempted to react rashly, by turning to drugs or alcohol or by losing their temper, this method tells them to come to a halt. Then they ask, "Am I hungry, angry, lonely, or tired?"

When any of these feelings weigh on us, our weakness shows as we fall back into bad habits again. But these are not only questions about physical hunger or tiredness. Emotional hunger and mental exhaustion are as disruptive to good habits as their physical counterparts!

As Paul says, "Faith comes from hearing" (Romans 10:17). Observe how often these moments of weakness are mentioned in the New Testament. In Matthew's gospel alone, Jesus blesses those who "hunger and thirst for righteousness" (5:6), addresses anger (5:21-26), encourages the lonely (28:20), and asks the tired to come to him (11:28-30).

This is where the Christian's habits of worship will make or break him. When we are in stressful situations, we tend to rely on what makes us who we are. Who we are deep inside becomes strong enough to get out, regardless of any safeguards we put in place to appear normal.

When we are not aware of where we are—physically, mentally, or emotionally—we tend to blame our shortcomings on our circumstances or those around us. We become snappy and short-tempered, we suffer a nervous breakdown, or we turn to destructive habits. In turn, we become unable to keep up with the demands of life because we are sleeping too much, watching too much television, or overusing social media.

The downward cycle continues because the more you do these things, the easier it is to get sucked back into them. We build a tolerance to sleep as we would to addictive chemicals like drugs. Social media becomes our opiate. We drown our sorrows in television.

These habits dull the pain but do not fix the problem! If the problem is being overburdened or emotionally starved, all these responses only leave you with less time to do what you need to do. We continue to be hungry, angry, lonely, and tired, and stop functioning as a light of the world. We are no different because we have little faith.

If our concern is to become more effective as Christians, we need a system to remind us where we are spiritually and where we need to be. That is what worship does! "Break thou the *bread* of life." "*Angry* words, oh let them never from the tongue unbridled slip." "I traveled down a *lonely* road and no one seemed to care. The burden on my *weary* back had bowed me to despair." These hymn lyrics remind us to H.A.L.T. where we are as they take us to where we need to be.

Continue singing these songs, and you will come to lyrics that offer the solution—how to arrive where we wish to be. "And I shall find my *peace*, my all in all." "'*Love* one another,' thus saith the Savior." "Be faithful weary pilgrim the morning I can see, just lift your cross and follow *close to me.*" We find the resolution for our hunger and frustration while we sing them!

In the conclusion of James' letter, he says, "If anyone among you is suffering, he must pray. If anyone is happy, he must sing" (5:13). These admonitions, however, don't preclude singing during suffering or prayer during happy times. Many Psalms were written and performed as laments and funeral dirges; likewise, prayers are not only offered in times of suffering. Paul says, "I thank my God for every memory of you at all times—in every prayer of mine on your behalf" (Philippians 1:3). Instead, James is calling us to worship God throughout all circumstances—as in 1:2-4. He does not mean, in those opening verses, they should rejoice only when they fall into various trials; rather, they should still rejoice even when they do.

Don't get me wrong; the major idea of singing praise and offering prayer is to give glory to God. These acts of worship also, however, make us aware of our perspectives and help us align and mold our perspectives into his. When we sing songs about how beautiful heaven will be or what Jesus endured for us, we take a step outside our timelines and into the eternal plan. When we pray about getting through a difficult time or give thanks for God's provision in the past, we remind ourselves he is in control.

We begin to examine life from God's perspective, become more aware of his presence and provision, and reaffirm our faithfulness to his covenant. Like all good habits, this takes practice. We will take these two habits of worship— prayer and singing—and tackle them one phase at a time.

## PHASE 1: PRAY LIKE DANIEL

> *"When Daniel knew the decree was enacted, he entered*
> *his house, opened the windows in his upper room toward*
> *Jerusalem, and bowed his knees three times per day, praying*
> *and thanking his God just as he had done before."*
> *—Daniel 6:10*

In Daniel 6, Darius signed a decree limiting all worship and prayer for the next 30 days to be directed to him alone. Daniel responded by doing something he rarely did—defying the king's edict.

Long before that day, he began going to God in prayer. This was not some last-ditch effort from him—a shot in the dark to keep him out of trouble. It was a demonstration of his commitment!

This was proof of his hope for God, who rescued him from death when Nebuchadnezzar's army sacked Jerusalem. He exhibited evidence of devotion to God when he refused to eat Nebuchadnezzar's delicacies and when he told Belshazzar what the writing on the wall meant. Although each trial was something new and frightening, he had seen new and frightening things before and reacted the same way.

Remember how his three friends defied Nebuchadnezzar while asserting their faith did not depend on their fate? They said, "Our God can deliver us from your hand, but whether he does or not, we will not bow down to the idol you set up." Daniel had a "though" faith, as they did, and as Habakkuk did several years before. How do we develop one?

**Pray personally.** This is not a habit of learning a magic phrase and repeating it many times per day. Learning the habit of prayer involves learning to pray for what is on your mind and what you want to be on your mind at the time. In the case of our biblical models, only a few examples tell us what they prayed. In John 17, Jesus prays for his future and the futures of his disciples. He recalls the glory he had in heaven before the earth was created. He asks for unity and faithfulness among his disciples, "so they may all be one." In his prayer in the garden later that night, he prays for God to take away the cup, but he appends his perspective-aligning last request: "Let your will be done, not mine." He tells Peter earlier in the night that Satan has asked to sift the disciples like wheat (the plural "you" is used in Luke 22:31). So Jesus said he has prayed for Peter's faith not to abandon him but to lead him to strengthen the others. These prayers were personal and heartfelt, and the requests made in them were for things Jesus needed or felt concerned about at the time.

**Pray with thankfulness.** Paul talks about prayer candidly in his letter to the Philippians. It is easy for us to overlook the circumstances in which he wrote them the letter: He was imprisoned because of the gospel—because he did the right thing. At one time he enjoyed a flourishing ministry throughout Palestine, Syria, Asia Minor, and the Greek Peloponnese. Now confined to a cell, he is unable any longer to make the impact he once made. How does he respond? "I thank my God always for you, never ceasing to remember you in my prayers" (1:3-4). He lists several things for which he is thankful: the gospel was still being preached (1:18); Jesus set aside the throne of heaven to save us (2:5-11); Epaphroditus recovered from his illness (2:25-28); he had a prize to strive for in his future (3:14); and he always received what he needed to get by (4:10-13). Leading into chapter 4, he tells them, "Always rejoice in the Lord—I'll say it again: Rejoice! Make your yielding nature visible to all people because the Lord is nearby. Do not be worried about anything. No, in every circumstance, with prayer and supplication offered with thankfulness, make your requests known to God. Then the peace of God that surpasses all understanding will guard your hearts and minds in Christ Jesus." Give thanks no matter how bad your situation is now. God has given us something far greater than what we're going through (and after this life, he will give the full amount of it).

**Pray with an open mind.** When we pray, as James said in 1:6, we must do so with faith—but this does not mean we can claim what we want God to give us and it will be so. Put yourself into the shoes of the man in Acts 3 who sat by the entrance to the temple complex begging for money. Imagine you were never able to walk—not as a toddler, or as a child, or as a teenager watching your friends run and play. Now you're an adult in a society with no official public welfare system. The only way you can make ends meet is by sitting in a high-traffic area and asking for money from everyone who walks by. When Peter and John come up, you catch Peter's eye.

"Can you spare some money, sir?" But instead of what you ask, he gives you what you need. After this encounter, you can walk. Not only that, but you can also run, jump, and praise God wherever you want! Will God give us the most comfortable outcome in life because we prayed? Not necessarily! Remember, Jesus prayed three times for the hour to pass by him and the cup to pass from him, and it did not happen. Paul asked three times for his thorn in the flesh to be removed, and it was not granted. Be faithful and trust God, but also be open to receiving a different answer than the one you expected. Trust him when you get an answer that does not bring you the news you wanted. Like Daniel's friends, admit that while God can make things better, he is not obligated. Our faith must not depend on our fate.

## PHASE 2: PRAISE LIKE DAVID

*"Nevertheless, the people of God find themselves again
and again in the interim between God's promise and the
fulfillment of the promise. That interim is when faith is put
to the test, for there are no unambiguous proofs that God
has spoken and that God is in control of
the human situation."*
*—Bernhard W. Anderson*[2]

When we think of a "new song," our minds might go to Revelation, where John records the hosts of heaven singing a new song to the Lamb. But David sings about "new songs" in many psalms, usually when he asks God to intervene. If God will come to the rescue, David says he will sing a new song to praise him.

As foreign as this concept might be to us, often a time of God's intervention occurs immediately before a new song is recorded in Scripture.

---

[2]Anderson, Bernhard W. Page 55 in *Out of the Depths: The Psalms Speak for Us Today.* Louisville: Westminster John Knox Press, 2000.

In Exodus 15, the Israelites sing about how they crossed the Red Sea on dry land and God's power annihilated Pharaoh's army. In Judges 5, Deborah and Barak sing about the fall of Sisera—a song they composed for that situation. According to the superscript, David composed Psalm 51 after Nathan the prophet came to tell him God knew of his sin with Bathsheba. A new song meant having survived one more threat to faith thanks to the power (or, in David's case, the mercy) of God. These new accomplishments needed to be praised with new music.

**Sing what you feel.** No one is asking you to be a Mozart here. At times, the songs of praise you know from singing with the church will be the most appropriate way to worship. Sometimes the song could be simpler. In the 1994 movie *Little Rascals*, Buckwheat is given a dollar and responds with an impromptu song. "I got a dollar! I got a dollar! I got a dollar, hey, hey, hey, hey!" Now, he wasn't nominated for a Grammy for that song, but it communicated his thankfulness and joy. Whether you compose the lyrics yourself or sing the "old hits," make sure your song describes the state of your spirit, emotions, and mind. Like the addict struggling against chemical dependency, come to a halt and recognize what is happening and why.

**Sing what you want to feel.** This is not a contradiction of the first point. Like Jesus' prayer in the garden, this is singing's version of "Let your will be done, not mine." I am not telling you to be dishonest or "fake it until you make it." Like David's psalm I mentioned a moment ago, use your song to ask for forgiveness, courage, strength, happiness, or whatever you need. Those are honest, heartfelt pleas. "Lord, I believe—help my unbelief!" When you sing, use the song to align your perspective with God's. Let its message teach you, encourage you, and remind you of the danger of being distracted by the wind and waves. Let the song bring your attention back to the Son of God so you do not lose heart.

# –III–

# VIRTUE

## FINDING OUR PURPOSE
## IN BECOMING LIKE HIM

*"Education without values, as useful as it is, seems rather to
make man a more clever devil."*
—C.S. Lewis

JOSEPH'S BROTHERS SOLD HIM INTO SLAVERY WHEN
he was just seventeen years old. By age thirty he worked for Pharaoh—not as
a slave but as a trusted advisor and his second-in-command. The short distance
in our Bible between Genesis chapters 37 and 39 might cause us to miss that
when Joseph entered the service of Pharaoh, he had spent more than 40% of his
life either in undeserved servitude or imprisonment.

What would cause many of us to become embittered against our families
or against God instead refined him and gave him an opportunity to save many
lives. He would tell his brothers, "Do not be afraid [of retribution]; am I in
God's position? What you did, you intended things to go badly for me, but God
intended goodness. He accomplished saving many people who are still alive."

Through all this Joseph does not ask, "What's in it for me?" or "When will
God improve my circumstances?" His only concern is for the hardships to
result in the praise of God. Even in regards to the situation—an invitation from
Potiphar's wife to "lie with me"—that put him into prison in Genesis 39, he asks,
"How could I do this thing and sin against God?" He is not so much concerned
about his reputation or his father's, and he does not cower at the thought of

disrespecting Potiphar. He only says he cannot sin against God.

The prophet Daniel had the same attitude. He entered captivity at a young age—perhaps as a teenager, since his prophecies continue for another seventy years. He lost his home, his family, and his freedom as he became a servant to Nebuchadnezzar, around 605 B.C. What is the first thing we see him do? He challenges the king's command to eat the delicacies from the king's table. He asks to be served vegetables and water instead.

Later, when his friends are told to bow before the statue Nebuchadnezzar set up in chapter 3, they refuse and say, "Our God can save us from your hand, king. But even if he doesn't, we will never bow down to the statue you have set up." Regardless of what they considered fair—regardless of their powerlessness in the face of the forces at work against them—these men kept their virtue intact.

Others had to learn the hard way that their behavior lacked virtue. Luke 15 tells us of the man with two sons, the younger of whom demands his inheritance early and runs off to spend it, enjoying his life untethered from all accountability. When he finds himself impoverished and malnourished, he considers why he is suffering so terribly. This self-inventory leads him on an arduous internal journey—a journey in which he comes to himself. Once he "arrives" and is aware of his reality, he immediately realizes what he needs to do. He goes back home, apologizes to his father, and asks for a job as a servant in his household since he no longer has rights to his father's property. He shows integrity, goes back to the one he hurt, and attempts to make amends.

In 1900, one of America's folk legends was made. John Jones—better known as Casey—was an engineer for the Illinois Central Railroad, known for his love of the job. A few years earlier, according to a 1939 biography by Fred Lee, Casey had turned control of the engine over to another engineer so he could do some maintenance before they stopped at the next station. While on the front of the engine, he noticed several children run out across the tracks ahead. All had time to get clear of the track except the last child, a little girl who stopped from fear. He crawled down onto the cowcatcher, reached out as far as he could, and pulled her to safety.

In April 1900, after working double shifts to cover for a sick engineer, Casey agreed to run a line back to Jackson, MS, from Memphis, TN. The train was late to arrive in Memphis, and he had more than an hour of time to make up if he was to avoid running late.

After the first three hours of the trip, despite having to make several stops to refill the water tank on the steam engine, he had made up all but about five minutes of his time.

Near train stations there were often sections of the track that split off to one side so a train could pull onto the side track and let another go by. That night at the Vaughan, MS, train station, there were actually two trains on the side track, and the total length was a few cars longer than the side track allowed. They would have to do a "saw by" to let another train pass: The stopped trains would move forward or backward to let a train past one end and then change direction to free up the other end for the passing train to get by.

For some reason, Casey was unaware the tracks ahead of him were occupied. The official report (which is disputed by several accounts) stated he ignored the flagman and the alert system, which should have warned him. Simeon Webb, who worked side by side with Jones that night, said there was no flagman until they passed what should have been the final warning signal. By then, they had no time to stop. They rounded the long left-hand turn, and Webb spotted the caboose on the track in front of them.

What happened next shows the character and courage of Casey Jones. He grabbed the brake handle and pulled back with one hand, and then he pulled the train whistle with the other. This warning gave people on his train and the stopped trains time to brace or get out of the way. He told Webb to jump when the train had slowed to a safe speed, while Jones stayed on the brake to make sure the train slowed as much as possible. By the time of impact, he had decreased the speed to approximately 35 miles per hour, minimizing the number of injuries from the inevitable crash.

Some reports say the engine crushed him when it derailed. Others say debris from the other train's caboose killed him. Everyone said he was the reason no one else was critically injured—because he held the brake and whistle rather than bracing for impact. His last act showed his character: He was a man who took seriously the responsibility for getting his passengers to their destinations, even at the expense of his life.

## WEATHER REPORT

*"Virtues are acquired through endeavor, which rests wholly*
*upon yourself. So, to praise others for their virtues can but*
*encourage one's own efforts."*
—*Thomas Paine*

Once the cold front and warm updraft begin to synergize and roll over one another, the updraft catches one section of rolling current and stands it up on its end. This causes the warm air not only to continue rising but also to spiral upward around the spinning cold air. As this happens, Doppler radar will pick up rotation in the atmosphere above the ground. This might not indicate a tornado touching down, but if such rotation continues, it is just a matter of time.

We might visualize the next four characteristics of 2 Peter 1:5-6 as this vortex in the atmosphere, or mesocyclone. The presence of these qualities (virtue, knowledge, self-control, and persistence) does not guarantee a world-flipping faith, but if conditions remain favorable, it will eventually.

Why is virtue part of the upward spiral? Let's define the four parts of this "spiritual mesocyclone" in simple terms, and in doing so, we will recognize a strong, overlapping connection from one to the next.

Virtue is the tendency to do what you know is right. Knowledge increases your understanding of what you should do. Self-control gives you the ability to do what you decide. Persistence ensures you keep the spiral going. So you learn what to do, bring yourself to do it, and make consistent improvement to your character. A deficiency in any of these four areas will cause you to stop growing in each of the others.

As we learned in the introduction, it would be dangerous to consider all these qualities from 2 Peter 1 to be habits alone. Each of them has an internal focus, a spiritual starting point, which habits cannot develop. For example, worship without the right motivation cannot produce faith any more than acts of kindness might cause you to like people.

At the same time, we learned in the previous chapter that an inactive faith doesn't save (James 2:14). These habits exist to complement the spiritual origin of each characteristic. Especially with virtue, we might massage our conscience by listing all the good things we do. This does not, however, mean we're virtuous.

Consider an athlete who does much for his community but is arrested for domestic abuse or sexual assault. What amount of charity work will make him seem like a "good person" in the public eye? The person who is good must have good morals while performing good actions. If morality is present first, it will refine itself through habit, as in the words of Aristotle: "Virtue comes about as a result of habit. We become righteous by doing righteous acts, self-controlled by doing acts of self-control, brave by doing brave acts."

Lest we misunderstand him, he also says, "Virtue makes the goal right, practical wisdom [makes] the things leading to the goal [right]." Virtue is how we know what purpose is right, and practical wisdom involves the planning and habits we adopt to achieve that purpose.

So, saying moral excellence *results* from habit differs from saying moral excellence *is* a habit. It is a cycle. Habits increase our ability, and virtue increases our responsibility. Because of virtue, we invest in habits. Through habits, we strengthen our virtue.

## THE ESSENCE OF CHRISTIANITY

> *"Now the reason for common swearing is this:*
> *Men have not so much as the intention to please God in all*
> *their actions. Let a man but have so much piety as to intend*
> *to please God in all the actions of his life,*
> *and then he will never swear more."*
> —William Law

Let me challenge your perspectives a little.

Human nature pressures us into seeing other people differently and makes us resistant to change, but Jesus' ministry (and the New Testament written by his earliest disciples) is full of commands to treat others like yourself and to be different from what your bodily desires want you to be. It doesn't matter if "that's just who I am." Paul says, "It is no longer I who lives but Christ" (Galatians 2:20).

The essence of being a Christian is overcoming our nature with God's.

In Hebrews 11:1 we find the definition, "Faith is the confirmation of what is hoped for." The word translated "confirmation" refers to a defining factor, without which we could no longer define it as such.[1] Having children makes one a parent. Buying a house makes one a homeowner. Being hired makes one an employee. The presence of a single factor changes your status. As faith is the essence of hope, virtue is the essence of a Christian life. Without it, can we call ourselves Christians? Unfortunately, many do!

Reread the quote from William Law at the beginning of this section. We might make argument after argument about what words are curse words or whether curse words are really that bad, since the Bible never comes out and says what words we cannot say; however, if a minister, a child, or your grandmother is standing near you, do you suddenly feel the inclination to clean up your speech? That shows you feel guilty about them hearing you use those words! That you are able to hold back in front of certain people means you have the ability not to use those words ever. If the knowledge is present, and the ability is there, the only reason you fail to do the right thing is you do not intend to!

It is hard enough to apply this concept to the words we say, but what about our overall behavior? We experience a paradigm shift when we stop acting based on "what is a sin" and start acting based on "what most pleases God."

I first encountered this concept in 2005, and it shook my confidence in my faith. I needed shaking! I was a young minister in my last year of college and had begun my first work in a local church. Because I was only twenty-one years old, I had the tendency to think I had everything figured out. Very few people my age were in ministry—and all the older church members reminded me of this constantly. I felt like a star—a celebrity ready to perform on a world stage. In just one brief chapter (four pages) of his book *A Serious Call to a Devout and Holy Life*, however, William Law confronted me because my heart was in the wrong ZIP code. If I wanted to be who I thought myself to be, a lot of soul-searching and soul-fixing lay in store!

---

[1] In Greek antiquity, this was a technical term used to describe the precipitate in a liquid solution, similar to the remains of coffee grounds and tea leaves you might find in the bottom of a cup. It is proof of what was there, like faith is proof of hope and virtue is proof of Christianity.

A statement he made later in that chapter might be the first seed of the book you are now reading. He said, "Now, who can be reckoned a Christian while lacking this genuine sincere intention? Yet if it generally existed among Christians, it would change the whole face of the world. True piety and exemplary holiness would be as common and visible as buying and selling or any trade in life."[2]

## PETER'S VIRTUE IS DIFFERENT BUT NOT NEW

*"Virtue's the paint that can make wrinkles shine."*
*—Edward Young*

Peter wrote his letter using words that were not new to his readers, even though their scarcity in the New Testament might lead us to think otherwise. When these concepts are present, often the vocabulary used by New Testament authors is different. *Virtue* is one of those words, and so are *godliness, kindness,* and *self-control.* Multiple terms are used to describe these traits, and each author tends toward using his own preferred term to express the same concept. Furthermore, *virtue* and *kindness* are used differently in the New Testament than in other ancient Greek literature. We will cover the difference in the usages of *kindness* in its chapter.

Virtue is listed in Philippians 4:8 among the concepts on which we should concentrate and in 2 Peter 1:3 in reference to the powerful works of God—"his own glory and virtue." In this passage, Peter uses the word the way the Greeks would to describe the valiant deeds of their heroes and gods. A virtue set this hero apart and made them like no one else. This is a quick litmus test we can use to examine whether we live virtuously: something sets us apart from all the pretenders and wannabes.

This word's Hebrew counterpart is used in Old Testament poetry to express the concept of power. Psalm 33:17 speaks of the false hope in a horse's significant

---

[2]Law, William, Page 22 of A Serious Call to a Devout and Holy Life: Edited and Abridged for the Modern Reader. Louisville, Kentucky: Westminster John Knox Press.

*power*. Psalm 18:40 praises God for supplying *courage* for battle. Ruth 4:11 is a well-wish for Boaz to be *influential* in his region and city. Isaiah 8:4 decries the soon-to-be seizure of Samaria's *wealth*. Proverbs 31:10 (and the praise in verse 29) sing to the wife who *surpasses* them all. These are all words we employ to describe someone who is not like anyone else—someone who is set apart. If your behavior blends in with everyone else, virtue is missing.

Now, lest we become arrogant in our attempts to surpass them all, remember God called us to *his* virtue and glory. Peter wrote of this in 1 Peter 4:11: "Anyone who speaks should speak as they are God's messages. Anyone who serves should serve as God has supplied the strength so that in every way God will be glorified through Jesus the Messiah." Our acts of moral courage and distinguishing behavior must point to God. Our lights shine so people see our good actions and praise our Father who is in heaven (Matthew 5:16).

Our tendency is to fall to one of two extremes—we either do many great things and call attention to ourselves, sounding a trumpet so others see us, or we refrain from action so we don't call attention to ourselves. We try to fly under the radar. If our actions do not draw attention and focus that attention on God, we are not exercising the virtue that Peter prescribes.

Christian virtue differs critically from the classical philosophers' idea. To Aristotle, for example, virtue existed to bring happiness and well-being to someone. In *Eudemian Ethics*, Aristotle explains why a person would suffer for a cause that others find senseless or ignorant: "All virtue is based on intentional choice—and by this we mean that it makes one decide everything based on something. That something is what is good." His idea of happiness was a satisfaction that derived from within—a drive to get up each morning and face the day with purpose. Something has virtue if it moves someone toward his own idea of happiness. If music makes you happy, for example, practicing piano is an act of virtue because it is part of your path to excellence.

Peter has already used the word virtue in verse 3, giving us a different context for the source of its meaning. God's virtue stands as the model by which we are to measure our own. Our who, our why, and our where find their answer in Him. We must be holy because He is holy (1 Peter 1:16). We must forgive because He forgives (Ephesians 4:32). We must endure unfair treatment because he did, leaving us a template so we could walk in his footprints (1 Peter 2:21). Our virtue—our supreme good—is wrapped up in the one who called us to his own virtue.

As we proceed through the rest of the characteristics in 2 Peter 1:5-7, emulating God is what drives each step. Through this process we come to know God and his will, exercise restraint as we conform to it, and persist in it daily. Then this purpose manifests in an attitude of subjection to God—almost becoming worship itself—in godliness. It takes on fairness and mercy in our dealings with our brothers and sisters—in kindness. Finally, it matures into the one word John said was equivalent to God: love. Virtue is not something we can put to the side as we move on down the buffet line. It is not something we should require only from the spiritual elite or think is beyond our grasp. If your faith is ineffective—if you bear little or no fruit— missing this one step could be the reason. Now is the time to bring every thought captive to our obedience to Christ.

## What more do I lack?

*"The virtues are lost in self-interest*
*as rivers are lost in the sea."*
—Franklin D. Roosevelt

Let's look again at the young man from Luke 18. One day when Jesus was teaching, a young, influential man who wanted to be part of the new kingdom approached him. He asked, "Good teacher, what must I do to inherit eternal life?" Jesus responded with a list of commandments, to which the young man said, "I have done all these since I was a boy. What more do I lack?"

Jesus responded, "Go sell everything you own and give the money to the poor. Then come follow me."

The young man went away upset because he was very wealthy.

"What more do I lack?" is a question that can bring us some humiliating answers. This question is one God calls us to ask ourselves daily. Paul would later write, "Examine yourselves to determine whether you are in the faith" (2 Corinthians 13:5).

Jesus spoke allegories in Luke 14:28-33 about two people who failed to do this. One man, a king, was ready to go to war when he realized the enemy outnumbered him two to one. At the last minute, he had to withdraw his attack and seek terms of peace because he did not first take inventory—or, in Jesus' terms, "count the cost." The other man was looking to build a tower but had to stop halfway through because he did not have the resources to finish.

This kind of self-examination is a painful process. It's frightening to face all the moral faults you have—to realize how far you have to go to be on solid ground with God. This fear causes us to make a "hopeful commitment" that in the end does not mean much.

I'm reminded of an episode of The Office titled "The Boat," in which Oscar asks Kevin to keep a secret. "Can you do this, Kevin?" Kevin puts his hand on Oscar's shoulder and says, "I really want to. Whatever happens, always remember that."

When we decide to do anything, if we are not virtuous, we sound just like Kevin. We make rash commitments, overbook ourselves, and then struggle to follow through with what we promise. It's not our intention to fall short, but it becomes our habit.

As a result, we cause unforeseen problems for others who expect us to follow through. We are forced to take care of ourselves rather than those in our care. We promise to bring rain, but we are blown around by the wind. We should bear fruit, but we only look the part. We are driven by our circumstances as our embarrassing secrets wash up on the shore. Though we should guide others like lights, we are never in the same place twice. These are poignant descriptions of a life without virtue, and they are not original to me. Jude said them in verses 12-13 of his letter. How frightening is the possibility we could be so dangerous and deceptive?

This happens in weather systems, too.

There is a type of storm called a "low-precipitation super cell," which has a tall anvil cloud, usually indicative of tornadoes, but it does not have enough rotation in its mesocyclone to produce the rain, hail, downdraft, or funnel that a typical anvil cloud will produce. These occur commonly in areas west of the Mississippi River, and concerned citizens often report them to weather stations, but the radar detects what is (or rather what is missing) inside the cloud, not what it appears to be on the outside. As Samuel was told in 1 Samuel 16:7, "Man sees what is visible, but the Lord sees the heart."

Sin will restrict and weaken our upward spiral, and one of the frightening things about sin is how it can blindside us. In Galatians 6:1, when Paul tells those who are spiritual to restore someone who is caught in some kind of sin, he is not referring to being caught in the act. The word has to do with being ensnared— caught in a trap that was set out in advance. The sin blindsided this man like a diagnosis of terminal disease!

Much like we need to have regular physical check-ups to remain aware of illnesses at war within our bodies, Christians must examine themselves for any kind of abnormality of virtue.

## STARTING TO LIVE  <u>M</u>  W    D (MEDITATE)

> *"Without a searching and fearless moral inventory, most*
> *of us have found that the faith which really works in daily*
> *living is still out of reach."*
> *—Bill W.*

Central to the virtuous life is a willingness to examine oneself under a merciless microscope. James tells us, "If anyone is a hearer of the word and not a doer, he is like a man gazing at his natural reflection in a mirror. He goes away and immediately forgets what kind of man he was. But the one who turns back to look into the perfect law of liberty—not being a forgetful hearer but one who does the work—will be blessed in what he does" (James 1:23-25).

This word for "turn back to look" is the same word used of John when he and Peter ran to the tomb when Mary said Jesus was alive. John ran up to the entrance and *stooped* to peek inside. Peter himself uses the same word in I Peter 1:12 to describe the behavior of angels who wanted to know how the gospel plan would work itself out in Christ as the prophets spoke of things "into which angels wanted to *take a look.*"

James is not recommending we take just a quick glance—in fact, that was the mistake the do-nothing man made. His gaze into the mirror was quick and forgetful. The one who is blessed is the one who stops to stare into it, soaking up whatever information he can find.

This is the habit of meditation. We take a long look at who we are and what shortcomings we have in Phase 1. Then we tackle them courageously, overcoming them in Phase 2 by showing integrity.

## PHASE 1: SELF-INVENTORY

The first phase of this chapter's habit can be a hard one. We take an immense amount of care to ignore our shortcomings. One of the biggest biases affecting decision-making is confirmation bias. When we think something is right, all the evidence agrees with us. When we come across evidence that disagrees, we can explain it away.

Our effectiveness at this point depends on our ability to see ourselves unapologetically in the floodlight of the Word of God. Therefore, it is essential for us to open our eyes as we look into ourselves. Exercise the same amount of care you would if you were looking to buy a car or house or hire a babysitter. Do not accept the lies you are inclined to tell yourself, like "Everyone struggles with this" or "I'm doing much better than others are." These kinds of self-deceit convince us that fixing our shortcomings will not be worth the effort and inconvenience it will bring.

**Make a list.** In Alcoholics Anonymous, this step involves making a written list of all your destructive habits—as many as you can name—and how those have hurt people in each facet of your life. Even if you are not an alcoholic, this exercise can help you. What about your temper? Your materialism? Your desire for inappropriate sexual gratification? Make a list. It will hurt—that is part of this. You are finally telling yourself a truth everyone in your life knows except you. If you do this courageously and for the reason of making your life right, it will have the effect we talked about in chapter one, which Paul described in 2 Corinthians 7: a godly sorrow that will not be regretted. It is like a surgical procedure—causing a temporary pain without which there will be no recovery.

**Check it twice.** When this level of self-inventory is new to you, begin with the ready-made lists in the New Testament, but remember my warning from earlier in the chapter: Our tendency is to pick and choose as if we were at a buffet. This will get you nowhere except the false safety of your confirmation bias. Take the items in a given list one by one, and for each item, evaluate honestly how well you do with it. Some lists to get you started are 1 Corinthians 13:4-8, Galatians 5:19-23, Romans 1:20-32, and Ephesians 4:25-5:32. This will take considerable time, if you do it correctly.

**Make a recurring commitment to personal inventory.** It is not enough to do this one time or even for a year or so only. Phase 1 needs to be a regular part of your routine. Virtue is your compass, and this is how you calibrate it. Virtue is your knife, and this is how you sharpen it. Paul says in Romans 12:2, "Do not be conformed to the world—be transformed by renewing your mind so you can determine what is the good, pleasing, and perfect will of God." This must become the new norm!

## PHASE 2: SHOW INTEGRITY

Once you realize your moral deficiencies, the time comes to make a second display of courage by facing them.

Our confirmation bias has an ugly third cousin—the Fundamental Attribution Error. This bias downplays our shortcomings while placing more blame on others for theirs. In fact, precisely this error of judgment was what Jesus addressed when he said, "Do not tell your neighbor, 'Let me remove the splinter from your eye,' when look—a log is coming out of yours!" (Matthew 7:4).

When you know something is wrong and do nothing about it, you are the kind of person Jesus condemned in Matthew 7—a hypocrite. No matter how small those sins look when you find them, remember your first inclination will be to underestimate them. Do not underestimate them!

**Make amends.** Like someone working through the Twelve Steps of Alcoholics Anonymous, you must recognize the consequences of your character flaws. Think about those closest to you—family, friends, coworkers, etc.—and list how your failings have hurt each one. Once you complete this list, go to each person and acknowledge your fault and that you know you have hurt them. Make a commitment to them to be better because you value your relationship with them more than these faults in your character.

**Check your fruit.** Once you know the fruit that should come from your actions, keep watching to ensure it grows and ripens. Are you becoming more patient and forgiving? Are you exercising restraint regarding your impulses and temper? Jesus said in Matthew 7:17, "Every good tree produces good fruit, and the bad tree produces bad fruit." Do not let your heart lie to you—check the fruit and know the tree!

**Clear yourself of guilt.** In 2 Corinthians 7:11, Paul describes for his readers the path down which their God-ward grief had taken them. The first thing grief produced was diligence. He continues by saying it drove them to answer for what they had done, be angry at their sin, and be afraid to let it happen again. Grief produced a desire—even a passion—to prevent the sin's recurrence, and then it rendered a verdict of deserved self-punishment. After they had done this, Paul said, "In every way you have proven to have cleared yourselves regarding this matter." Without integrity, we will either pardon ourselves unjustly or punish ourselves unjustly for every misdeed. Examine it, give it the proper level of punishment, and let the guilt go. Even though it might take time to rebuild others' trust, do not add imaginary debt against yourself.

By now, especially if you have been a Christian for a long time, you might realize how difficult it is to have the powerful working faith Peter says is required. If, however, you train your mind with the habits of these first three chapters, you will soon be decisive and self-aware with much less effort. As we continue into the next two chapters, those habits will be necessary to help you come to know God's will better and submit yourself to it. By then, we will be halfway through Peter's list of qualities, and the effect on your life will have begun to unfold!

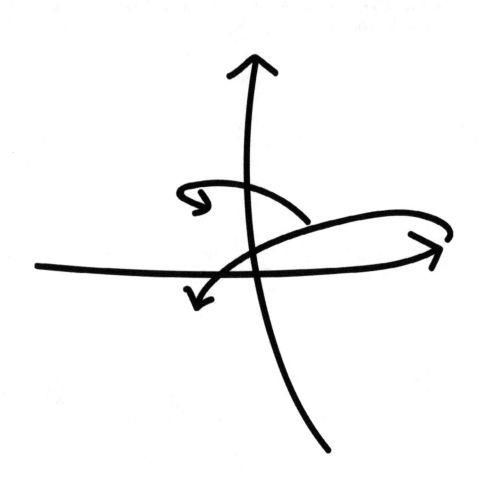

# –IV–

# KNOWLEDGE

## EDUCATION AND EXPERIENCE
## REQUIRED

*"Facts don't care about your feelings."*
—Ben Shapiro

AFTER DECADES OF HUMILIATION FOLLOWING THE destruction of the temple and Jerusalem in 585 B.C., things began to look promising for the former people of Judah. In 539, Cyrus the Great, a Persian king who began to rule over the Median Empire ten years prior, conquered and put an end to the Babylonian Empire. Though they were still a conquered people, Judah and several other nations received permission to return to their homelands and rebuild.

Several years later, King Artaxerxes commissioned Ezra to lead a convoy of Israelites (whoever wanted to go) back to Jerusalem to offer a sacrifice to God based on the Law of Moses. You can read this decree in Ezra 7:12-26. Like many other heroes of the Hebrew Bible, Ezra found favor with the king because "the hand of the Lord his God was on him."

In verse 10 we learn the reason for God's favor: "Ezra decided in his heart to study the Lord's Law, to keep it, and to teach its tenets and regulations in Israel." Ezra's plan of action was simple: first, Decide; second, Learn; third, Do; and fourth, Teach. Notice how closely this progression correlates with the habit phases from chapter one; we find "decide" and "do" in our chapter on diligence!

Now, logically it would not make sense to proceed in any different order.

How could a man do what he has never learned? What happens when we try to teach what we have not learned?

Diligence requires us to learn. Although we might say *study* refers to gaining knowledge, it is more than that. When we talk about a person being *studious*, that description includes diligence. This is why some translations tell us to "Study to" show ourselves approved, and others tell us to "Be diligent to" show ourselves approved (2 Timothy 2:15). We must learn it *and* do it.

In Hosea 4, the prophet brings God's complaint against his people with a devastating picture of imminent judgment. They had broken God's covenant and acted unfaithfully. They continued to worship God but did not keep his covenant. God's message includes in verse 6, "My people are dying from a lack of knowledge." God is saying Israel is starving to death, though not physically. They had no knowledge of God or his will!

Whenever we hear tragic news of a child dying because of a daycare's negligence, we respond with outrage—those childcare providers are unfit! Take those children to safety! Likewise, God responds with disapproval toward those who have been negligent in caring for his people: "Because you rejected knowledge, I reject you as a priest." They had been given an administration to care for God's people. As members of his covenant nation, the people had the opportunity to know God, but the priests did not fulfill their responsibility to distribute his Word to them—so he revoked the priests' license to provide care.

My nephew Eli is one of my real-life heroes. He was diagnosed with Type 1 Diabetes when he was seven years old. This means every meal or physical or emotional effort requires careful monitoring of the levels of glucose in his bloodstream. Thanks to modern technology, he now has a continuous glucose monitor, which gives him a real-time measure of those levels. This lets him know whether he needs to eat now or wait and what types of food he should eat. It tells him when he needs to take a break from physical activity and when he needs to supply his bloodstream with artificial insulin so his body can metabolize what he has eaten. For him, accurate and immediate knowledge of his glucose levels and whether ketones are present in his bloodstream is the difference between a "normal day" and a hospital stay.

It's not simple math, either. Insulin is measured in units equal to 1/100 of a milliliter (one teaspoon contains 493 units). Sensitivity to insulin varies per person, but for the sake of comparison, one unit of insulin will lower my nephew's blood glucose by seventy points. The recommended healthy range is from about 80-180—a variation of 1.5 units in Eli's case. This means if he were to miscalculate by just two percent of a milliliter, his blood glucose would be at a life-threatening level. He relies on nutritional labels, portion size estimation, and the calculation of insulin levels based on his individual sensitivity to insulin.

In a real, physical sense, the 1.25 million T1D patients in the United States could perish merely from a lack of knowledge, like the people of Judah in Hosea's day. They cannot disregard the information or let their feelings decide. They need to know.

## WEATHER REPORT

*"Any fool can know. The point is to understand."*
—*Albert Einstein*

In the previous chapter we began to observe the mesocyclone of powerful faith. This four-part spiral begins with virtue, which originates in the urgency of diligence and the direction of faith. Unquestionably, virtue is vital, but our virtue is limited by our understanding. As we grow in knowledge, our virtue is put to the test, stretched, and finally strengthened—not unlike the muscles of our physical bodies.

I mentioned William Law's observation that we do not have so much as the intention to please God with all our actions. How do we know whether God is pleased with our actions if we're not increasing in knowledge? Then, once we know, we must do what we have learned. The result is an increase in virtue. This is the upward spiral—the funnel in the sky that can eventually develop into world-changing power. We cannot break this chain in a single place without compromising the entire outcome!

The idea that "it's the thought that counts" is a gross miscalculation when it comes to our relationship with God. To have this mindset is to say God should be happy I thought about him. This puts us at the same level (at least) as God when that is nowhere close to the truth.

This is akin to baking a pie to take to your bank in place of this month's mortgage payment. You might think you are being thoughtful, but you are breaking the commitment you made when you signed the promissory note. You agreed at that time to pay on the bank's terms, so what you think is "good enough" is irrelevant. One might as well do the same for their future spouse on the day they are to be married instead of attending the ceremony. There are some situations where you must know what is required of you, and you must follow through as expected. Paul told the Roman Christians in his letter they were "without excuse" because the knowledge was out there—it was just being rejected (Romans 1:20-21).

Like virtue, the concept of knowledge was not new to the first-century Greco-Roman audience. The oracle at Delphi, where pagans would go to seek the will and guidance of the gods, was decorated with engraved maxims and proverbs. One of the most well-known, quoted by Socrates and recorded by Plato, was "Know yourself." For these philosophers, knowledge and reasoning (the *logos*, which John uses to describe Jesus) are the way to living the best possible life.

## A Rose by Any Other Name Is Not an Onion

In 2 Peter, knowledge most often is part of a larger phrase, "knowledge of the Lord and Savior." A specific knowledge is required here—not a mastery of the proverbs and philosophies of mankind since the beginning of history. Nevertheless, some people call the wrong things knowledge.

I remember a short-but-powerful lesson I heard from Ben Flatt while I was in college. He brought an onion up to the podium, and he said, "This is a rose. In an age when being cool is hot, and being bad is good, and being really great is wicked, this is a rose."[1] He proceeded to talk about the many ways we claim one thing to be so while we do the opposite or while the Bible has said the opposite.

He then quoted Isaiah 5:20, which reads: "Those who call evil good and good evil are in trouble, as are those who trade darkness for light and light for

---

[1] A transcript of this speech can be found on pages 63-64 in FHU Chapel Speeches. Vol. 3. Henderson, Tenn.: Hester Publications, 2004.

darkness, who trade bitter for sweet and sweet for bitter. They are in trouble who are wise from their own viewpoint and consider themselves to be intelligent." God's people at that time in Judah reveled in what they thought were great things, but their knowledge was their own—not God's.

This continued to be a problem for them because several centuries later Paul talked about their descendants: "They have a passion for God but not in regard to knowledge. Because they are ignorant of God's justice and try to establish their own, they have not submitted to God's justice—because the goal of the Law is Christ, resulting in justification by faith for everyone."

Knowledge has a destination—seeking God's approval. Anything else is pointless, as the book of Ecclesiastes echoes throughout. In 12:12-14 the author talks about the endless capacity for research and studying and then concludes, "The bottom line once everything has been heard is this: Revere God and keep his commands because this is everything as far as man is concerned." Any knowledge that talks us out of doing God's will is pointless.

Jesus also addresses this in Matthew 15: "Why do you sidestep God's command on account of your traditions? God said, 'Honor your father and mother' and 'Whoever speaks evil to a father or mother must be put to death.' But you say, 'If someone tells his father or mother, "What I would have owed to you is a gift offering [to God]," that man will not honor his father at all, and thus you nullify God's Word on account of your traditions." Jesus then quotes Isaiah, "There is no point to their worship of me because they teach lessons that are the commands of men."

I might believe it strongly. I might do it sincerely. This does not make it truth!

Jesus elsewhere said, "You experts in the Law [of Moses] are in trouble because you take away the key to knowledge. You do not enter into it yourselves, and you forbid others who try to enter it" (Luke 11:52). For several centuries these "experts" had developed philosophies, safeguards, and traditions to help ensure they and the people kept the Law—but they were hemmed in by their protective walls to the extent they protected themselves *from* the Law! Their teaching was disguised as knowledge, but it enslaved them to misinformation. They needed to know the truth so it could free them (John 8:32).

On the night of the tornado, I was at work 30 miles away. I knew the storms were bad and heading toward Walnut, but the weather was nowhere near as bad where I was. Earlier that day, people commented on how dark and "bad" the weather looked outside. I told them, based on my childhood experience of another storm, the sky often appears to change color during a tornado—the red clay or greenery swirling through the air gives an eerie glow to the world!

I called my wife shortly after 5 p.m. from our break room at work to see whether it was bad enough that I should wait it out at the office. She didn't know what I should do, but the storm had been bad. At the last minute, she had gone to my sister's house, where they heard it pass by. Within two minutes of our conversation, she called me back and said my uncle had driven by our house—and it was gone.

When I got off the phone and was sure the worst had passed us, I started out the door to make my way home. I stepped out of the break room and overheard another employee say, "Oh wow, it destroyed that house next to the little church on the other side of Walnut." My house.

Think about how differently things could have unfolded. Imagine if the storm had destroyed the cell tower near my sister's home, and I had been unable to call my wife. I would not have known she was safe at my sister's house. What if my uncle had been unable to get word to me that my house had been destroyed? After trying unsuccessfully to call, I would have overheard about my house, and my knowledge would have been different. I would have known only that I could not contact my wife, my house was destroyed, and as far as I knew, she was at home.

Believe me, this was all I thought about for months afterward—even while decorating a Christmas tree for the first time the next year.

If the only thing that had been different, however, was the cell tower being destroyed, my wife and family would still have been fine, since they were not at home when the storm hit. The "reality" that would have formed in my mind WOULD NOT HAVE BEEN reality. This is the risk we take when we rely too much on what we believe or feel to be true but don't dig into the Scriptures so we can know the truth. Knowledge must be based on truth, not troubles; fact, not feelings; information, not inferences; worship, not worries.

At times we focus too much on our concerns. I know what awful things I did and what terrible thoughts I entertained. I know I am supposed to be holy, but I also know I am going to struggle if I try to do better. You see, my heart condemns me before I have the chance to stand trial. To me, it might be a foregone conclusion—like so many other things I try in life, Christian faithfulness will be a temporary obsession, and in the end I will still be me. With this attitude, I might give up before I've started!

John addresses this in 1 John 3:18-20. He talks about the end goal (that we love in action and truth—not just in the spoken word) before saying, "By this we know we are of the truth and convince our hearts in his presence, because even if our hearts condemn us, God is greater than our hearts and knows everything." In other words, my heart does not qualify to be the jury for my trial. God knows everything my mind and heart know. If he wants to forgive me, what business do I have not to forgive myself? If he wants to give me the benefit of the doubt regarding whether I will stay faithful, why should I disqualify myself before I try?

## TRUE KNOWLEDGE IS INTIMACY

*"Real knowledge is to know the extent of one's ignorance."*
—*Confucius*

From the earliest few chapters of Genesis and Matthew, we recognize the word "know" as a euphemism for the intimate relationship between a husband and wife (Adam and Eve in Genesis, Joseph and Mary in Matthew). Now this is only an extension of its meaning, but it shows the word means more than an awareness of information. Remember, the same was true of faith, as explained in chapter two. Being faithful to your marriage means more than believing your spouse exists! Likewise, knowing God and his will is more than understanding and acknowledging facts.

Faithfulness is a relationship fanned into flame by years of time spent together. There might be times in your past when your faith has helped you get through difficulty. Sometimes you recognize what happened in your life to be the result of providence and mercy—the answer to your prayers.

One of the greatest parts of long relationships—both friendships and marriages—are those little things you see that remind you of the other person. Someone in the room might hum a song your friend liked. You might see a trailer for a movie your husband or wife would really like to watch. A restaurant might serve a pie that smells like the one your grandmother used to make. Even if they are not literally with you in that instant, they are there. You might experience hundreds of such little reminders each day that you love one another. This might lead you to call or message them or stop and reflect on them.

This is where true knowledge of God can make itself known to us. Consider those moments every day when we are reminded of what God has done. When something happens, do our thoughts immediately go to one verse or another where the Bible describes the appropriate response we should give? If so, we possess a knowledge that brings us intimacy with God. In Titus 1:16 Paul warns Titus of people whose minds and consciences were defiled: "They claim to know God, but they disown him by their actions. They are disgusting, disobedient, and unqualified for any good work." To know God is to identify with him and remember him through our actions. I cannot do that while living a lifestyle that is opposed to his teaching (see Titus 2 for details).

This is a prominent theme in 1 John as well. In 2:3 he says, "By this we know we know him—because we keep his commands. Whoever says, 'I know him' and does not keep his commands is a liar and the truth is not with him."

A quick test is to ask yourself how many times you were reminded of God today. How many times did you feel motivated spontaneously to pray, as you might feel the urge to call a friend or your spouse? How many times did you reflect on something you studied in Scripture, something you were reminded of by your everyday life? Your answers will reveal how intimate your relationship with God is. Do you really know Him? Does what you know bring you closer to him? If not, then that knowledge will not help you develop a powerful faith!

## TRUE KNOWLEDGE IS EXPERIENCE

The book of Hebrews talks about the need for us to grow in understanding. In chapter 5 the author points out that Jesus learned obedience and had several qualities in common with Melchizedek. The author had more to say but stopped because his recipients were not ready to listen. Verses 12-13 say, "Although by this time you ought to be teachers, you again need someone to teach you the basic tenets of God's teachings, and you have come to need milk instead of solid food, because whoever takes in milk is inexperienced with the message of righteousness."

Many critical professions in this world require both advanced degrees and internships. If you wish to become a doctor or nurse, for example, you must complete the classroom requirements and then spend terms in residency, working under professionals who mentor you. Inexperienced engineers can have a designation called "Engineer in Training" that allows them to work under the direction of someone with the designation of "Professional Engineer."

The practical side of Christianity (especially ministry) was once a struggle for me to comprehend. I went to a Christian university and graduated with a B.A. degree in Bible, so I gained a lot of experience talking about what faith *should* be, but somehow I missed the lesson of *how* to live it each day. When I began my first work in ministry, I was convinced that several aspects of my job were outside my job description, and my responsibility was to help everyone else to become philosophers of the faith. I would have benefited from some time spent with a mentor during those early years.

I later had the opportunity to work on a ministry team with an experienced minister and mentors who served as elders and deacons for the congregation. My first work was when I became a preacher; my second made me a minister. How many things I would have done differently if my second work had been able to prepare me for that first one!

It is one thing to know the Ten Commandments and quote memory verses; it is another to know how to keep your integrity intact throughout the constant bombardment from pressures within the church, detractors outside of it, and the risk of burnout that always threatens a person who serves the Lord passionately.

The same could be said of parenting. The advice given by those who have not raised children often seems far removed from the reality of what parents actually go through, so parents tend to ask advice from other parents. If you want Christian knowledge, studying will only take you so far. You must practice Christian behavior and experience obedience. If you need help with something new that you have never experienced, go to a Christian who has experienced it—not someone who thinks he knows best but hasn't lived it. Practice daily, improve on your habits, and be a little better each day. Knowledge requires both learning and doing!

## IT'S NOT WHAT YOU KNOW; IT'S WHY

> *"You will ever remember that all the end of study is to make*
> *you a good man and a useful citizen. This will ever be the*
> *sum total of the advice of your affectionate father."*
> —John Adams

For some people, knowledge is the goal, not the means. They take pride in how much they know and take every opportunity to show others just how much that is! Knowledge, for them, is something to show off. They view it as a path toward acceptance and respect—and that should be our first clue it is not the knowledge Peter is talking about.

In chapter two we noted Peter's use of a *sorites*, a device that begins with a foundation for the other items on the list. It ends with something that is a goal for every item on the list. In our particular *sorites*, if your "knowledge" does not result in love, you're pursuing the wrong knowledge.

Reread the last sentence! Paul contested this attitude in 1 Corinthians 8. In the first verse he says, "We know we all possess knowledge—knowledge puffs up; love builds up. If someone thinks he knows something, he does not yet know what he needs to know. But if he loves God, he will be known by him." If your knowledge leads you to arrogance, you have the wrong knowledge.

The knowledge that makes a difference is the knowledge that drives you to love and goes much deeper than facts. Its range of meaning also includes understanding, which can refer to facts and truths but also refers to the response we give when we know those things.

For example, if I talk about being an "understanding spouse" I am not referring to the things I know! However, because I know what my wife needs, what causes her to worry, and what buttons I could push to upset her, I show love by acting kindly in accordance with that knowledge. This is Peter's meaning when he urges husbands and wives to "dwell with one another according to knowledge" (I Peter 3:7). This understanding is what leads to kindness and forgiveness. It is the awareness that stands guard over what we hold dear. Without true knowledge, we rely too much on our confidence.

At the other extreme, we might overlook red flags that would otherwise prevent us from going forward, as in unhealthy relationships. If we know someone is dangerous and harmful to us but we convince ourselves we can handle it—or worse, that we deserve it—we are not acting based on knowledge.

True knowledge also supplements faith. When we reflect on our struggles in the past and are reminded of God's faithfulness, we gain courage to increase our faithfulness to him.

Consider the father in John 4 who came to Jesus with a pretty big ask. This father had traveled from Capernaum to Cana—a thirty-mile trek—in hopes Jesus would take the trip back with him to Judea to heal his son. When Jesus says instead, "Go, your son will live," we are told, "The man believed what Jesus told him and went." As he approached his home, his servants ran to meet him to say his son recovered. He asked what time it had happened, and when they told him the time, "the father knew—that was the time when Jesus told him, 'Your son will live.'" This is not an inkling or a feeling. Because he knew what Jesus did, "he himself believed, as well as all his household."

Through this newfound knowledge, he went from one level of faith (no one thinks a thirty-mile walking journey was taken on a whim) to another, and in the process he brought his entire household with him. How? I'm sure he told them, "That's exactly the time I was talking to Jesus, when he said my son would live." Now they had knowledge, and they increased in faith.

This is part of Paul's argument in Romans 1-3. In 1:17 we are told, "The righteousness of God is revealed in [the gospel] by faith for faith." It begins at faith and results in more faith. Continue reading into the third chapter, and he expands on that idea in verse 21. "Now the righteousness of God is revealed separate from the Law, though the Law and Prophets attest to it. But the righteousness of God [is revealed] through faith in Jesus Christ for all who believe."

The process is centered on and driven by faith. Where does that faith originate in Paul's estimation? Look at 10:13-17: "For all who call on the name of the Lord will be saved; but how will they call on one whom they have never believed? How will they believe unless they hear about him? How will they hear without someone announcing it?" We observe a progression from increasing in knowledge to increasing in faith until Paul concludes, "So faith comes from what is heard, and what is heard comes from the Message of Christ." When we don't seek to understand, faith becomes stagnant. We become ignorant of God's will. We have no basis for kindness and will never be able to love the way God does.

## STARTING TO LIVE **M** **W** **ED** (EXAMINE)

> *"Human behavior flows from three main sources:*
> *desire, emotion, and knowledge."*
> *—Plato*

## PHASE 1: LEARN

**Read scripture following a regular plan.** Based on the length of a typical audio Bible (around 75 hours), you could read through the whole Bible in a year in 15 minutes per day. As much as we like to make excuses about finding the time to read the Bible, if we are not able to say we recently read through the entire Bible, it is only because we did not made a regular habit of reading it. I challenge you to tell me you can't set aside 15 minutes per day in your schedule! If you have a commute to work, an audio Bible can do wonders for your habit. If you drive a thirty-minute round trip to work, you could finish the Bible in about seven months, even if that was the only time you listened to it! If you read the New Testament only, that is about 17 hours for most audio Bibles; you would need just over a month if you spent 30 minutes per day reading or listening! One of the pitfalls many of us meet in our Bible study is the tendency to focus on a favorite passage or on one or two verses at a time. There is a place for such study, but it should not be your primary method. If you want to understand the message of the Bible, you need to read all of it. How quickly you do so will depend on the time you can devote each day. The satisfaction of reading the whole Bible is only one of the benefits. When you have read Isaiah multiple times over the course of several years, you will start seeing how Matthew relies on him quite a bit. When you read Ezekiel, Daniel, and Zechariah and become accustomed to the imagery of their prophecies, Revelation begins to make a lot more sense. You begin to recognize a dialogue among the authors about important topics—faith versus works, grace versus obedience, and justice versus mercy. If we focus only on passages we hold dear, we instead close our minds to a much better understanding of the gospel!

**Keep it new.** When you read the Bible through a translation, you get the meaning of the original language's text—but as it is for anyone who speaks English as a second language, there are times when any translation will struggle for the best way to express the original concept. There are always trade-offs in translation. Some versions trade proper English fluidity for a more word-for-word precision. Some focus more on the thought presented in the original language and use the best English expression to communicate that thought. Both philosophies have their strengths and weaknesses, and we do ourselves a disservice when we latch onto just one of them. I'm not saying you will be deceived if you use only one translation![2] However, when you use only one translation, you are limited to that translation committee's ability with the original language and English, as well as to its decision-making process. If instead you use a different translation each time you read through the Bible, you will receive a much fuller representation of what the original language intended. Also, hearing the same information in different words will cause it to sound fresh to your ears even after reading the Bible dozens of times. I mentioned in the first tip that audio Bibles are helpful; if you prefer to listen instead of read, you can use one of several smartphone apps that let you access audio versions of all kinds. Dozens of them are available for English translations,

---

[2]In the words of the KJV translators in 1611, "The very meanest [mediocre] translation of the Bible in English...containeth the word of God, nay, is the word of God."

including most of the popular ones. Some are even dramatized with different voices for each part: When you listen to Matthew, it is not the same voice as when you listen to Mark, and when James and John converse with Jesus, you hear three different speakers!

**Learn secular skills, too.** While knowledge of the Bible is essential to your productivity as a Christian, the principle of being studious and eager to learn should apply to the other parts of your life as well. If you are stubborn and refuse to listen at school or at work, what does that say about your attitude toward your current level of knowledge? Paul said, "So the one who thinks he stands must be careful not to fall" (1 Corinthians 10:12). Proverbs 12:1 states bluntly, "Whoever loves discipline loves knowledge, but whoever looks down on correction is stupid." Be sure to learn skills relevant to your roles in life—marriage, family, career, etc. Treat those roles like a houseplant—if they are not flourishing, make sure you planted the seed, watered it, and cared for it in the way it needs (just as some plants need direct sunlight while others will struggle in it).

## Phase 2: Teach

**Teach what you know.** Look again at the pronouncement of judgment in Hosea 4:6: "Because you rejected knowledge, I reject you." It is vital for us to remember it was the priests' job to provide spiritual guidance to Israel. Israel was dying from a lack of knowledge, and the priests were at fault. Israel failed the test because no one was teaching them. We see a similar rebuke in Hebrews 5:11-12. It is not enough to know for yourself; when you have made learning a habit, you must then develop the habit of teaching what you know. Perhaps our biggest reason for failure to teach is the fear we do not know enough to do the job correctly. Rather than lamenting you are not as qualified as someone else, focus on what you *can* teach.

**A three-question method.** Are you a Christian? How did you come to be one? Why was it important for you to do that? If you can answer these three questions with solid biblical reasoning, you are ready to teach someone to become a Christian. For example, you ask, "Are you a Christian?" They respond that they are or are not. If they are, ask them how they came to be one. As they relay the story to you, use sound biblical teaching to evaluate with them whether they truly obeyed according to the New Testament or fell short due to misunderstanding. If they do not claim to be a Christian, use solid biblical reasoning for why it is important, trying to encourage them to follow through with it. It is important for you to be able to show them from scripture so it does not come across as your interpretation versus theirs. Since faith comes from hearing, and that comes from the Word, keep your focus on winning the soul, not the argument! If you cannot confidently answer these three questions, focus on finding those biblical answers first.

**Balance confidence with an open mind.** Remember, from the beginning of this chapter, the order of actions Ezra took and continue to follow his pattern as you grow into an effective teacher. Decide, learn, do, and teach. As you grow in your knowledge and experience, and as you develop the other behaviors prescribed in 2 Peter 1, you will be able to teach more. You will be like someone who successfully loses weight—those who are seeking similar success will come to you. You will be able to mentor and guide them along the path to attain diligence, virtue, self-control, and the other characteristics, so they can be fruitful too. This is more than the sharing of information, however. For example, in the next chapter we will see that learning self-control has little to do with intellect and much to do with determination. You will not become a good teacher of the gospel because you happen to be good at teaching—you will become one by faithfully deciding to be virtuous as you learn and do what that virtue requires. This does not mean we discount faith—faith is each of these things.

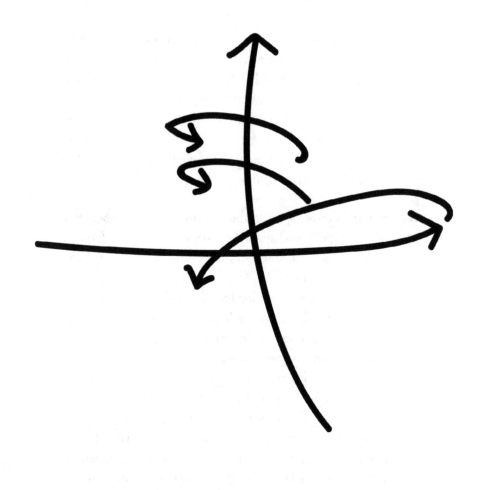

# –V–
# SELF-CONTROL

## YOU CAN'T CHOOSE A MASTER
## UNTIL YOU ARE YOUR MASTER

*"Discipline is choosing between what you want now
and what you want most."*
—Abraham Lincoln

IN 1 SAMUEL 13:14, GOD TELLS SAUL HE IS GOING TO appoint a king "after my own heart." Does this mean he would be perfect like God? Absolutely not! The atrocities this future king would commit involving Bathsheba and Uriah are unquestionably terrible. The arrogance he displayed when he numbered his army was irreverent as well. Before those moral failures, however, we saw some brilliant flashes of devotion to God and to God's anointed king.

Almost as soon as David entered the public eye, he rose quickly to prominence. With each feat he either overshadowed King Saul's achievements or illuminated the king's shortcomings. When Saul was tormented by an evil spirit, David's music made him feel better. When Saul and his army were paralyzed with fear because of Goliath and the Philistines, David (likely a teenager) matter-of-factly picked up five stones and faced the giant without armor—and won. When Israel won battles, people would sing the praises of the king—but those praises underscored David's superiority: "Saul has killed thousands but David tens of thousands!" (1 Samuel 18:7).

Saul began to be jealous and sought to kill David. On one occasion he threw his spear at David, trying to pin him to the wall. Then he thought better of it—instead of murdering David, he could use the sword of the Philistines by challenging David to an impossible act of valor in exchange for marrying the king's daughter. David not only accomplished that impossible task, he doubled it. He had charisma, popularity, courage, skill, and now a legitimate connection to the throne of Israel.

Saul decided to take matters back into his own hands. David had to flee for his life while Saul pursued him through the wilderness. David went from living in the king's palace to taking refuge in caves.

While David was hiding in one such cave at En-Gedi, Saul came after him with a force of three thousand men. Saul happened to enter the cave where David was hiding and stepped aside to use the restroom, giving David a prime opportunity to kill the king and end the terror. David, instead, cut a piece of fabric from Saul's clothing, which he presented to Saul to prove he had the opportunity to kill the king and did not.

Later, in 1 Samuel 26, David came upon the camp of Saul's army—again three thousand strong. This time the army was asleep. David and one of his trusted soldiers slipped into the camp and swiped Saul's spear and water jug. David then called out to the army to reprimand them for failing to protect Saul. David again had the opportunity to take Saul's life but didn't.

Imagine the exhaustion David must have felt after running from Saul all that time. How unnerving would it be, looking over your shoulder, expecting an arrow or spear to be hurtling toward you at any time? Would you be justified if you were to kill the one trying to kill you? If you did, your closest friend is next in line for the throne, and you might even have a claim to it yourself because the prophet Samuel anointed you, and you married into the king's family.

David not only resisted but also repeated the same refrain—"I will not strike down the Lord's anointed king." His integrity throughout this ordeal remained intact because he knew what was right (knowledge) and why he needed to do it (virtue)—and then he did it (self-control).

The British Medical Journal published an article by Vladislav Rogozov and Neil Bermel titled "Autoappendicectomy in the Antarctic."[1] Rogozov's father,

---

[1] Rogozov, Vladislav, and Neil Bermel. "Autoappendicectomy in the Antarctic." BMJ: British

Leonid, had been part of an expeditionary team to the Antarctic from 1960-1962. The team opened their base of operations in February 1961 in preparation for a year of being cut off from the outside world. Near the end of April, Leonid began feeling ill and running a fever. Telltale pain and inflammation in his abdomen signaled appendicitis, and surgery would be his only hope of survival. The problem was that he was the surgeon and the only one on the team with formal medical training. He weighed his options for a few days before deciding to operate—on himself.

He employed the other members of his team. They sterilized the room, removed all equipment not essential to the procedure, and propped him up on his left hip in what he called a "half-sitting position." He gave one a syringe and showed him what to do to restore the surgeon's consciousness if he were to pass out. He gave one the implements to hold open the incision. He gave another a mirror so he could see better as he cut on himself, though Leonid later wrote, "The mirror helps, but it also hinders—after all, it's showing things backwards. I work mostly by touch."

At 2 a.m. May 1 he began the procedure; two hours later, he finished sewing up the wound. After seven days he was able to remove his own stitches, and he was back to work with the team a few days after that.

It's one thing to have the precise control over one's hands needed to operate on patients. It is another altogether to maintain such control when you are feverish, sleep-deprived, under the influence of local anesthetics, and unable to step around the bed to get a better perspective! In his words, though, "When I picked up the needle with the novocaine and gave myself the first injection, somehow I automatically switched into operating mode, and from that point, I didn't notice anything else."

Rogozov, like David, trained himself to the point where he didn't consider the option to give up. His decision had been made, he knew the risks, and the only thing left was to do what needed to be done. To us, what they did seems to be supernatural and amazing, but they "didn't notice anything else." Their strength came from an inner power. Where we might be tempted to give up hope or give in to our impulses, they did what came naturally.

---

Medical Journal 339, no. 7735 (2009): 1420-1422.

We tend to misunderstand self-control as restrictive, but the opposite is true. We might talk about the difficulty of eating healthy and exercising, but what about when your doctor says you might only have a couple of years to live if you do not change your eating habits? Both situations require you to take control of your diet, but in one you also get longevity and quality of life, as well as the freedom to go and do what you would love to do. Without discipline your hand is forced. This applies to finances, raising children, and even keeping your house clean. By trying to hold on to your freedom, you end up having no choice.[2] In the words of Jesus, "Whoever wants to save their life will lose it" (Matthew 6:25).

Without discipline, if you were Rogozov, you would only be able to say, "I'm going to die here because I need a surgeon and tools." In fact, even though the circumstances were in no way optimal, he had everything pertaining to saving his life, as we have everything pertaining to life and godliness.

I'm going to warn you now—this chapter will not be an easy one to read. However, gaining a mastery of yourself will make all the difference between making the goal and making excuses—between becoming the victor or the victim.

## WEATHER REPORT

*"He who has power over himself*
*has power over his greatest enemy."*
—Matshona Dhilwayo

I grouped self-control into the mesocyclone section because it is part of a closely-knit group of characteristics that rotate together to lift your faith like helicopter rotors. As I mentioned in chapter three, these qualities Peter commands are not new—several of them, in fact, were part of Greek philosophy centuries before Jesus walked the earth. Aristotle said, "We must treat each of the two (self-control and consistency) neither as identical with [the spectrum

---

[2] I was introduced to this by Jocko Willink and Leif Babin in their book *Extreme Ownership: How U.S. Navy Seals Lead and Win.* You should read their book.

of] virtue and wickedness nor as belonging to another family." Aristotle used a different word from Peter, but his point is the same: You cannot separate self-control or persistence from virtue. The quartet of virtue, knowledge, self-control, and persistence are as essential for the productive Christian's life as faith is to the four of them. Without virtue, self-control is stubbornness. Without knowledge, it is ignorance. Without persistence, it is a phase.

Learning self-control has little to do with intellect and everything to do with power over your impulses and reactions. Consider that Jesus "learned obedience" (Hebrews 5:8). This does not mean cognitive learning, because Jesus was present at creation! When the human body was created, he was part of the process. He was there when the radial nerve was stretched out between the bones of the arm and wrist, connecting the hand to the brain. Because of this nerve, we can feed ourselves, hold our children, and use pens, tools, and other instruments. Jesus did not need instruction on how the nervous system works—but when a nail was driven into his wrist, severing the radial nerve, he felt pain like any of us would. He could have called twelve legions of angels to prevent that torture, but by refraining, he learned obedience through what he suffered. He didn't learn information but what submission means—to let God's will be done and not his own.

This restraint is the power behind Jesus' words in Luke 17:6-10. He had taught his students to be careful to forgive one another of wrongdoing. When they assume this to be a matter of immense faith and ask for enough to be able to do it, he says, "If your faith is even the size of a mustard seed, you would say to the fig tree, 'Be uprooted and planted into the sea' and it would obey you." In other words, this is not a question of the *amount* of faith. It is a question of *substance*: "Do I have faith to begin with if I cannot exercise enough control over myself to forgive?"

This is why self-control is a frightening concept to many people. We do not trust ourselves to be strong when the need arises. We see flashes of brilliance and potential, but our failures and weaknesses are much more obvious to us. As discouraging as this might be for us, people have always been this way. When Paul was speaking before Felix in Acts 24:25, we are told, "As [Paul] was discussing righteousness, self-control, and the coming judgment, Felix became afraid and responded, 'Go away for now—when I get an opportunity I will summon you.'" Felix had invited Paul to speak on repeated occasions over the course of two years, but this topic hit too close to home. It is generic enough—controlling oneself—but what it entails will drive many of us reading lists of Christian virtues in the New Testament to skip over self-control like it's the mystery casserole at a potluck meal.

Understand this: If you want a powerful faith, you first must maintain power over yourself. Self-control is the only word in Peter's list that has power in its range of meaning—do not skip this one! You see, self-control refers to an inner strength. This includes controlling oneself but also refers to being a master of one's environment.

Picture the football player who is able to break tackles to gain many yards after first contact or the pitcher who routinely throws a baseball within a target of less than four square feet at close to a hundred miles per hour. Such skill truly involves mastery of self but also of the obstacles they face and the implements they use. Like Rogozov with his surgical tools, their daily practice of these movements means they now possess an automatically consistent precision.

Hebrews 5:14 applies as much here as it did in the chapter on knowledge—solid foods belong to those who "because they used them had senses that were trained to distinguish between good and evil." Being born with an innate talent for sports or medicine is not enough. NBA player Kevin Durant said in an interview that a former coach taught him, "Hard work beats talent when talent fails to work hard." The determination to make something happen—to take control—is a greater factor than the gifts you were born with. Now is the time to let go of the powerless thoughts of what we are not and what we cannot do. Today is the day to take the wheel and take control.

## THE HARSH TRUTH ABOUT SELF-INDULGENCE

*"The man with no self-control may be compared to the proverb, 'When water chokes someone, what are they to wash it down with?'"*
*—Aristotle*

A supplemented faith, even in a small dose, is effective. It will continue to affect our thinking and behavior as long as it is present, as a teaspoon of yeast is enough to leaven a pound of flour. If you struggle to maintain control of yourself, the issue is not your faith being too weak; the issue is that you have not applied faith to your impulses and responses. You will not fix the problem by learning more but instead by acting on faith. Paul says, "Everything that does not come from faith is sin." This is your chapterly reminder: Faith is the basis of each characteristic in 2 Peter 1. For a Christian's faith to be effective and productive, it must be supplemented with self-control.

The opposite is true, too. For your faith to be ineffective, all you need is a lack of control. This is what Aristotle's proverb means—if your problem is lack of control, nothing will fix you. There will be no godliness, no persistence, no love, no faithfulness—and there is nothing you can do to develop those things without having control.

Jesus condemned the scribes and Pharisees as hypocrites multiple times, especially in the week leading up to his crucifixion. "You are in trouble!" he says in Matthew 23:25. "You cleanse the outside of the cup and dish, but inside they are full of greed and lack of control. You blind Pharisee—clean the inside of the cup first so its outside can truly become clean."

This calls back to Haggai 2:12-14, when God sent the prophet to the priests with a pair of questions: "What if someone is carrying in his pocket meat that was sanctified, and it touches bread, stew, wine, oil, or another kind of food; does what was touched become sanctified?" They said no. The second question was, "If someone is defiled because they came in contact with a dead body, and they touch one of these, does the touched food become defiled?" They said yes. Then he gave the punchline: "So is the case with this nation in front of me, and so is everything their hands do—even what they sacrifice is defiled."

Wrong is the notion that we can offset bad behavior on Friday or Saturday by worshiping a little harder Sunday morning. If the hands offering worship are unholy, so is the worship they offer. If you do not learn to master your impulses, any chance of your faith being productive is canceled—and remember, you will be known by your fruit, so either gain control or lose your soul.

This begins with making ourselves aware that we make this choice in everything we do. How we react to our environments and whether we give in to our impulses will determine our outcome.

Learn from Cain. In Genesis 4, he is upset and jealous because God accepted Abel's sacrifice and not his own. God asked him point blank: "If you do well, will you not be accepted? But if you do not do well, look—sin is hiding behind your door. It wants you, but you must overcome." In his case, Cain did not respond by "doing well." He continued doing what he had already done, stewing over his jealousy and resentment. This eventually caused his rage to boil over, and he killed his brother.

Now, lest we think this was an accident or he "made one bad decision," John explains his motive: "Why did he kill him? Because his actions were evil, and his brother's actions were good" (1 John 3:12). He didn't restrain himself from his bad behavior and let his lack of control sign over his fate. John used him to illustrate a proof of what he had just said in verses 7-10: "Little children, do not let anyone deceive you—whoever makes a practice of doing what is right is righteous as [Jesus] is righteous. Whoever makes a practice of sin is from the devil because the devil has made a practice of sinning since the beginning."

He goes on to say, "By this it is clear which ones are God's children and which ones are the devil's children—anyone who does not make a practice of doing what is right does not belong to God, and neither does the one who does not love his brother." Paul's statement about knowledge—that if our knowledge does not result in love it is the wrong kind—is the same statement John now makes about our actions. Unless we can control ourselves, we cannot be God's children. This is our harsh truth.

Paul weighs in on self-control as well. In Romans 7:25 he makes a statement we might misunderstand to mean we are going to serve both God and sin (one with our mind and one with our flesh); however, this contradicts both what he says in Romans 6 and what Jesus says in Matthew 6—no one can serve two masters. Romans 6:16 reads, "Do you not realize that to whomever you submit yourselves in obedience as slaves, you are slaves to the one you obey? This is true whether you obey sin, which leads to death, or obedience [to God] which leads to justification."

In verses 19-23 he speaks of their slavery to sin and flesh in the past tense, saying, "But since you were set free from sin and entered the servitude of God, you have fruit resulting in holiness, the goal of which is eternal life." So he cannot be saying in chapter 7 that we are OK serving both the flesh and the mind or spirit. He says we are still being *commanded* by sin in our bodies. We hear its voice. The pull is still present. We have the desire to be loyal to sin. But as Cain was advised, we must overcome.

Continue reading Romans from 7:25 to 8:16, and you will see Paul come to the same conclusion as John. In 8:8-9, "Those who live by the flesh are unable to please God, but you are not of the flesh—you are of the Spirit, if God's Spirit truly dwells in you." In verse 12 he adds, "We are not obligated to the flesh so as to live by the flesh, because if you live by the flesh, you are going to die. But if you put to death the practices of the body by the Spirit, you will live." Finally in verse 16 he says, "The Spirit himself concurs with our spirit—we are God's children."

What is the bottom line? If you do not have self-control, you have nothing. I cannot surrender control of my body to the Lord if I do not have control of myself. If that happens to apply to you, everything hinges on obtaining control.

Paul's advice on how to be empowered to do this was to employ the Lord's armor. In Ephesians 6:10-20, how many terms refer to power or being able to do something? Looking at the first few verses we find, "Finally, be *empowered* by the Lord and by the *strength* of his *might*. Clothe yourselves with God's full armor so you *may be able* to stand up to the devil's schemes ... Because of this, take on God's full armor so you *may be able* to resist in that evil day and remain standing after accomplishing everything." Gaining control and being empowered requires us to equip ourselves with tools that work.

## HAVING A TOOL DOESN'T MEAN YOU CAN FIX IT

*"With great power comes great responsibility."*
—*Stan Lee*

If we do not utilize the proper tools, more work is required to achieve the same level of control.

I remember the truck I drove when I first obtained my driver's license. The power steering system had a leak somewhere, so periodically it would stop working. I could still turn the steering wheel, but it required much more effort.

The truck also, however, leaked brake fluid—and I had to be sure not to let those levels drop because no amount of strength pushing a brake pedal could stop a vehicle with no brake fluid! The absence of preparation, likewise, can make some things more difficult and others impossible.

A hammer is a useful tool with many functions, but its usefulness is dependent on what needs to be done. Do you need to attach multiple pieces of wood to one another and cover them with carpet? Then yes, a hammer will do nicely. Did you lock your car door with the keys inside and need to find a way to get in? I wouldn't suggest the hammer in that case! While you will get the desired result, it will bring undesired consequences.

The same is true of knowledge as a tool. Knowing something is one thing, but using knowledge wisely is the key. You might be aware of all the shortcomings of your spouse or children and be tempted to use that hammer when you want to change their behavior. Just remember, you are opening the door by breaking the window.

Wait a minute—this isn't the chapter on knowledge! What does this have to do with self-control?

When we know something, often we have a compulsion to say it, especially when we are hurt, angry, lonely, or tired (see the explanation of the H.A.L.T. method in chapter two—all these characteristics are interrelated). Be sure it is truly necessary to say what you know and that you don't just lack control over your tongue. Which is more important to you in the long run: getting what you want now or preserving your long-term relationship with the person?

When you choose to respond to a situation, there are three routes you might take:

1) You forget or neglect any knowledge you have about the situation.

2) You acknowledge those things in your mind but don't act on them.

3) You respond with integrity based on what you know.

Of those three routes, only one is both virtuous and wise; the third option allows you to do the best you know to do at the time. The difference between being wrong in a way you regret and being wrong in a way that leads to growth is how well you keep your integrity intact. You will learn over time, which means you will have been wrong many times. To avoid regret, use what you know wisely! It might well be the case that what you do or believe at a given time is not the truth, but acting based on virtue and knowledge will prevent you from later regretting, "If only I had remembered," or "I knew better than that." Those regrets are based on knowledge and virtue, but they are caused by a lack of control!

You will struggle at times—we all do. I've often heard someone remark, "Sorry, I'm on the struggle bus today." My response is usually, "Better to be on than under!" Even if we admit the struggle bus is not a good ride, real power comes once you realize you are behind the wheel! When we focus too much on the difficulty, we sometimes overlook the choices still available to us.

I came across a meme with the words, "I'm not just a passenger on the struggle bus—I'm the driver, owner, and mechanic!" Maybe I am the only one, but to me that indicates I am in a unique position to control this vehicle, use it for good, and make sure it stays in good condition. Do not deny the power of your choices!

In Proverbs 12 we are given several contrasts between wise and foolish people. Many of them involve control. In verse 13, the wicked man is ensnared by the things he says, and his freedom is taken away. On the other hand, the righteous person is able to escape capture by his words. Restraining himself leads to freedom.

Verse 16 says: "The unhappiness of a fool is known right away, but a wise person overlooks an insult." Inability to control our reactions puts us completely in the power of other people. How they treat us, any misfortune we face, and other external factors have absolute sovereignty over us until we can take back the steering wheel! And unless I can control myself, I can never submit myself to God.

## Starting to Live M OW ED (Overcome)

*"In reading the lives of great men, I have found that*
*the first victory they won was over themselves."*
—Harry Truman

## PHASE 1: CONTROL YOUR IMPULSES

**Learn your triggers.** One of the reasons we need to develop good habits is because we are prone to develop bad ones. They often develop as responses to triggers in our environment when we continue to respond in the same adverse ways. For example, if you go to lunch at the same time each day during the week, your tendency will be to eat lunch at the same time on weekends and off days. If you need a break at work, you might turn to the same type of drink or snack in the break room. When you feel the need for a break at home, you probably crave the same drink or snack. Our memories begin to associate 12:30 p.m. with "time to eat" and a Coke and Snickers with "I can no longer focus." In a more nefarious fashion, we begin to perform self-defeating behaviors based on triggers. Imagine your spouse uses "that look," and your habitual response is to raise your voice. That might trigger your spouse to walk off while you are talking. Before long, you have triggered each other into a big argument started by someone's impulse to give a look and someone else's triggered response. Learning your triggers will require you to take notes wherever you are, which is hard to remember but critical to do. Once you realize a trigger makes you act in a certain way, your success in changing your behavior depends on your ability to recognize and avoid or circumvent the trigger. This is where we struggle with sticking to diets, using that new planner, and keeping the house clean. ("I was going to do that, but Netflix...") We relinquish our control to our triggers and mourn our inability to change.

**Remove triggers for bad habits.** Wherever possible, remove those triggers that push you toward your bad habits. For example, if you scream at everyone in the family every Sunday morning because no one gets ready on time and you are always late for worship, get up earlier. Set a firm time to begin getting ready. An extra fifteen or twenty minutes in the morning might be the difference between your children associating worship with yelling and anxiety or love and togetherness. If a certain app on your phone makes discipline difficult for you, delete it. Jesus said, "If your right hand offends you, cut it off and throw it away." In the same vein, if your phone causes you to fail, turn it off and put it away. It is better to go through life disconnected than to be connected and lose control. Sometimes this involves replacing bad triggers with good ones. If break time at work means you eat an unhealthy snack, replacing it with a healthy snack and a short brisk walk might help you to regain the focus you need. After a few days of consciously making this change, you will begin to associate taking a stroll with relaxing and refocusing your attention. Doing this every day instead of eating unhealthy snacks will make a huge difference in your long-term health.

**Remind yourself why.** There will be times when you will be tempted to go back to the way things were—back to the easy way. Changing your habits will not seem to be worth all the effort you put into it. In these times, especially, you need a reminder of why you need to make those changes. With your temper, the reason might be because you want to set a better example for your children or to make your spouse feel more loved and respected. If your goal is to improve your diet, perhaps the reason is to feel better or to be able to play with your children more easily. I created a note file (I use OneNote) that is simply an outline called "Why." I listed all the major roles I fill and note my long-term goals for each role. As a sub-point for each, I put the reason why. For example, under "father" I might put, "I will not raise my voice because I want my children to have me as an example when they think of their heavenly Father's love." Periodically I will review my progress on my goals, and this includes reminding myself of the reasons for each goal. This lets my virtue help my self-control when the latter is weak. The same is true for the other characteristics from this book—your faith can help you maintain self-control, and so can your love for your family. At times, raw diligence and persistence will save the day.

## PHASE 2: CONTROL YOUR RESPONSES

**Learn why others do what they do.** You might have heard sayings like, "When people gossip about you, that says more about them than about you." Just as our habits are often poor responses to triggers in our environment, so also is the undesirable behavior of other people in our lives. Is there a difficult person at work? Can you pinpoint any triggers that cause them to be difficult? For example, they might feel underappreciated, or their parent or spouse might be chronically ill. If you detect they feel underappreciated, and you make a special effort to go to them and thank them for what they do each day, what do you think that will do for their demeanor? If you occasionally ask about a family member of theirs who is sick, and you listen to them as they talk about it, what will that do? You would be amazed how much easier working with "difficult" people can be when you learn to give them good triggers. This is not about manipulation—do not treat them this way to make your day better. Treat them this way to make *their* day better. This is when you truly start having a direct impact on the people around you.

**Be aware when you are negatively triggering others.** This habit comes to maturity when you begin to recognize you are responsible for triggers that affect the people around you. You progress from the starting point, where you were controlled by your environment and how everyone treated you, to the point where you are master over yourself and have a profound impact on the habits of others. Imagine you have the power to prevent a big fight with your spouse. Would you take the opportunity? Say you're the spouse who gives "that look." Once you're aware of what makes you give "the look," you have the power to step in and break the cycle by refusing to give the look. What if, instead, you decided to be triggered positively? Maybe they need a hug. Maybe they need you to offer to do some cleaning or go out on a date. Guess what this does to your spouse's demeanor? Guess what it does to your potential for a big fight? The truth is, we do not need to imagine having the power to control ourselves, and we do not need to wonder what a better relationship would be like or how much better we would feel if we kept to our diet. We only need to be aware of those situations when we are susceptible to giving up control. Learn to recognize and break the cycle, and you will possess a power stronger than anything you have felt—power over self.

**Remember your power rests in your actions and reactions.** Since we do not control most of our circumstances or others' opinions of us, our helplessness is wrapped up in how much we let those external things affect what we do. Do not let your triggers force you to respond against your will. Remember the warning in Romans 8: If you do what the body wants, you become its slave. Only by putting to death your response to those compulsions can you serve God. I cannot change what has happened to me—only how I respond. When I give up my ability to respond in the way Jesus would, I also relinquish hope of ever becoming like him. "Do not throw away your confidence—it has a great reward" (Hebrews 10:35). Take control and save your soul!

# –VI–
# PERSISTENCE

## THE ANVIL CLOUD FORMS

*"I think and think for months and years. Ninety-nine times
the conclusion is false. The hundredth time I am right."*
—*Albert Einstein*

H E WAS THE EPITOME OF DEVOTION. HIS CHILDREN
knew of his love for God, and even though they were older now, he still
made a habit of offering sacrifices on their behalf. They were a close-knit family,
living comfortably in the land of Uz, where their father raised livestock and
managed a large household business. No one around was nearly as wealthy, and
yet, his community respected him as a man of integrity.

Then the unthinkable happened. Raiders invaded his pastures and took his
livestock, killing many of his servants. On the same day, fire from heaven (likely
lightning) came down and killed more livestock and servants. While the first
servant was reporting what had happened with the raiders, the second came up
to report the fire from heaven. While the second still spoke, a third came with
the worst news: All ten of Job's children had perished when wind destroyed the
house where they were eating.

Job went from being the wealthiest man in the East to being left with only
three servants, his wife, and his health. By the end of the second chapter, his
wife was not supportive, he developed painful boils from head to toe, and those
servants were no longer mentioned. What would they have been able to do,

anyway?

Three of Job's friends came to visit him, and his condition was so bad, none of them spoke for seven days.

Job lamented being born and begged for an audience with God so he could learn what he did to deserve such an awful series of events. He never got his answer. His friends took turns saying Job must be at fault. We do not know how long Job suffered in that condition, but some of what he endured could not be reversed—at least until the resurrection. In the closing chapters, God instructed Job to offer a prayer on behalf of his friends for their miserable comfort, and Job ended up with twice as much property as at the beginning, and ten children were born to him.

When James addressed a congregation that was being mistreated by wealthy members of society, he reminded them, "You have heard of Job's persistence and have seen God's result" (James 5:11). Those Christians probably also struggled to find reason in what they were suffering. They were working for wealthy landowners who deprived them of wages (5:4), beat some of them, and killed others (5:6). They needed help to keep their "eyes on the prize," and Job was the inspiration they needed.

In 1847, a boy was born to a Milan, Ohio, family. Early in life, he contracted scarlet fever and several ear infections that left him with a hearing impairment. At seven years old he was struggling to focus at school, often causing distractions in his classes. The note sent home to his parents said he was being difficult, so his mother took him out of school to educate him at home.

When he was twelve years old, he got a job on a train selling newspapers to railroad passengers. According to his accounts later in life, he used to set up chemical experiments on the train and once caught a baggage cart on fire. He even attributed some of his deafness to being hit on the head by the train conductor as a punishment for performing experiments on the train!

While working on the train, he saw an opportunity with the telegraphs that reported news to the train operators. He began writing his own newsletter and selling up-to-date news articles to passengers based on what he overheard. He was making $50 per week at age thirteen (worth about $1,500 today). He recognized early his knack for finding a need and developing a viable solution.

Eventually, he would apply those talents in becoming a professional inventor and securing more than one thousand patents in his lifetime, including those for a phonograph for recording and playing music; an inexpensive and long-lasting incandescent light bulb; a motion picture camera; and a car battery. The last sentence might have clued you into the name of this boy: Thomas Edison.

Like Edison, some people seem to be made for adversity. They can dig deeper when the well runs dry and find the strength to continue and prosper despite the difficulties they face. How difficult would it have been to achieve such brilliant success despite what the school system thought of Edison? What if his parents had not ensured he receive an excellent education at home? What if the train conductor had fired him, preventing him from discovering his ability to innovate? What if he let his impairments be an excuse not to try?

Instead, he looked at his obstacles as temporary problems to solve. With one innovation after another, he made his life and the lives of others better. He began working because his mother could not and his father had lost his job, and in the process of his career, he started the General Electric company that even today is one of the largest employers in the United States.

## WEATHER REPORT

> "Making your mark on the world is hard. If it were easy,
> everybody would do it. But it's not. It takes patience, it takes
> commitment, and it comes with plenty of failure
> along the way."
> —Barack Obama

If you have ever witnessed a tornado firsthand, several things were probably inscribed into your memory. One of the first memories people mention is the sound. Oh, that terrible roar! I remember one from my childhood. I witnessed the sound, but something else stuck with me—the color of the sky. Because we were in an area with a lot of grass and trees, the entire sky looked green—like an apocalyptic movie!

The shape of the tornado's cloud is also distinctive—towering high above the surrounding clouds (because of the mesocyclone) and with a large projection coming out of the front like an anvil. This is where persistence finds itself in our image. As the cold front blows against the warm updraft of air, and the spiral continues to whirl around itself repeatedly, the rest of the cloud takes shape.

## WHERE PERSISTENCE BEGINS

We live in a world governed by natural laws. So many wondrous things occur in nature that we cannot explain, and the purpose of studying science—for several millennia—has been to solve those mysteries.

One of my favorite stories involves Greek mathematician Archimedes in an incident that supposedly took place around 250 B.C. Archimedes was told by the king of Syracuse to determine whether the crown the king had purchased was pure gold or made from cheaper metals; however, the king did not want the crown to be destroyed during testing, so Archimedes was not to break or melt it down. According to Vitruvius, Archimedes struggled to provide the king's answer for quite some time.

One night, as he prepared a bath, he observed how much the water level rose over the side of the tub as he got in and continued to rise as he sat lower in the water. Recognizing this was because the volume of his body was displacing an equal volume of water, he realized he could solve his problem by measuring how much water was displaced for an equal weight of pure gold and pure silver (the silver was less dense, so more volume was needed for the same weight, and more water would be displaced).

Elated by this discovery, he jumped out of the bath and ran naked out the door and down the street shouting, "Eureka!" (which is Greek for "I've found it!"). When he performed the test, the "gold" crown displaced more water than the pure gold weight did, proving the crown to be a forgery.

Sometime in history, someone learned that if you melt gold with fire, the pure gold sinks to the bottom, and you can scrape the dross off the top. In 1 Peter 1:7, Peter says that as fire purifies gold, testing purifies faith and produces "praise, glory, and honor when Jesus Christ appears." We cannot leave our salvation to chance because we would get those results only by destroying the crown. Once

Jesus appears, if we pass the test, we do, and if we don't, we don't. By then, it will be too late to make a difference!

James provides the solution for us in James 1:2-3: "Consider it a complete joy, my brothers, when you fall into various trials, because you understand testing your faith produces persistence." Eureka! We determine our faith to be true if our trials lead us to become persistent. Paul agrees persistence is a product of testing faith, saying in Romans 5:3, "We are proud of our afflictions because we know affliction produces persistence." In Romans 15:4 he tells us another place persistence comes from: "What was written before was written for our instruction so that by persistence and encouragement from the Scriptures we might have hope."

We recognize a pattern emerging, especially in the letter to the Romans, the basis of which is that knowledge of the Word of God must come first. Knowledge leads to faith in 10:17 and encouragement in 15:4. Both are prerequisites for persistence! In 2:7 Paul says that persistence in "good works" (self-control) and a pursuit of "glory, honor, and immortality" (virtue) will lead to eternal life. Persistence is inseparable from the storm because it fuels the other characteristics. It requires faith and increases faith; it requires virtue and increases virtue; it requires knowledge and increases knowledge.

## WHERE PERSISTENCE GOES

Persistence also bears fruit of its own. Let's revisit Luke's retelling of the Parable of the Sower in Luke 8:15: "But the [seeds] in the good soil—these are the ones who hear the message with a good heart, take hold of it, and produce fruit with persistence." James 1:4 agrees: "Persistence must have its complete work, so you become complete and whole, lacking nothing."

Paul says, "Persistence produces proven character, and character produces hope" (Romans 5:4). Paul talks about hope throughout Romans, often mentioning it together with persistence: "We are saved by this hope [the redemption of our bodies], but hope in something visible is not really hope— who hopes for what they see? But if we hope for something we do not see, we wait for it persistently" (8:24-25). "Celebrate in hope; be persistent in affliction"

(12:12).

As Jesus has said repeatedly, "You will recognize them by their fruits." We must take the time again for a potentially uncomfortable self-examination. Have I received the message of Christ, taken hold of it, and taken the message to a new generation of soil? Or are there holes in my faith or character—evidence I am lacking something? Is my hope failing?

This kind of self-reflection is necessary if we wish to determine what the crown is made of in a nondestructive way. In three passages Jesus says, "The one who persists to the end—that one will be saved." In all three passages (Matthew 10:22 and 24:13 and Mark 13:13), he is addressing his followers before his betrayal, and he is talking about the persecutions they will endure for his name in the coming years. Luke 21:19 is similar: "You will win your lives by your persistence." Paul listed this characteristic first among the evidence proving whether someone is a servant of God in 2 Corinthians 6:4. Do you see it in yourself?

## ROME WAS NOT BUILT IN A DAY, BUT IT WAS BUILT EVERY DAY

> *"I've missed more than nine thousand shots in my career.*
> *I've lost almost three hundred games. Twenty-six times I've*
> *been trusted to take the game-winning shot and missed.*
> *I've failed over and over and over again in my life.*
> *And that is why I succeed."*
> —Michael Jordan

An impatient person might receive encouragement that "Rome was not built in a day." In fact, the city was founded in 753 B.C., and with each generation (especially during the imperial era), Rome grew in both size and innovation. Each emperor built his own luxurious residence, and crews at work within the city expanded its walls generation after generation until its destruction 1,200 years later. Because the Romans built their roads and much of the architecture to superior standards, many of them are still standing two millennia later.

We might be tempted to expect success immediately, but that is rarely a reasonable goal. For example, when we try to lose weight, we need to remember we did not gain it overnight. We did not rack up our debt in one day. Sometimes the changes were unnoticeable from day to day, and as we try to reverse the process, the same will be true of our progress. There will be times when we seem to plateau and do not come closer to the finish line. One day we will, though. "So we must not become tired of doing what is good because in due time we will harvest as long as we do not give up" (Galatians 6:9).

## THE REASONS FOR STRUGGLE ARE AS IMPORTANT AS THE REALITY

*"This life's hard, but it's harder if you're stupid."*

We must be careful not to confuse struggle with endurance.

I've seen the quote above attributed to John Wayne, but the earliest I can find it being used was in a 1970 novel by George Higgins called *The Friends of Eddie Coyle*.[1] Sometimes we take pride in knowing how much difficulty we have overcome while ignoring that we have caused many of our difficulties!

During my time as a youth minister, I took part in several summer camps and weekend youth rallies. During these, I regularly witnessed teenagers bragging about staying up all night, only to beg for energy drinks to get through the next day. By the afternoon following their all-nighter, they were miserable with a headache, not wanting to engage with the group the rest of the night. It was not a feat of persistence that allowed them to stay awake the entire second day—they only did so despite themselves!

Peter did not pretend all difficulty was the same. He says in 1 Peter 2:19-20: "This is grace, when because of an awareness of God someone puts up with the grief of suffering unfairly. Now what glory is there in showing persistence when you commit sin and are punished? But if you show persistence after you do what is good and suffer, this is grace before God." Peter is using two terms (grace and

---

[1] John Wayne was in the movie based on this novel, but his character did not say this line.

glory) that have to do with showing favor to a person.

We are familiar with grace—the opportunity God gives us through the gospel to become his children because of the death, burial, and resurrection of Christ. Glory is a more secular idea. Many of our translations use the word *credit* here, but this was the term for the fame valiant warriors would strive to earn. It was their esteem and reputation among the people, like how they used the word virtue before the era of philosophers. The public recognized these heroes for their acclaim, but Peter warns them not to take pride in their struggle when the struggle is from their own doing! There is no valor in that. Persistence only has value when it is connected with the other qualities in 2 Peter 1:5-7. Without them, it is stubbornness.

## BE SMART ABOUT YOUR GOALS

A problem many of us have in being persistent is the tendency to be "lost at sea." We are not aware of whether we are making progress toward our goal, what we need to do to succeed, or whether we are achieving our primary purpose. If this is you, maybe part of the reason is you need to rethink how you set your goals.

In 1981 George Doran first used what he called the SMART Goal Evaluation Method, which sets guidelines for creating goals that give you the greatest chance of success. This method lays out criteria indicating SMART goals are **S**pecific, **M**easurable, **A**ttainable, **R**elevant and **T**imely.

Goals should be *specific*. A goal is not profitable if we do not have a way to define success. For example, I might set a goal of being a better Christian or a better spouse. What exactly does that mean? I need to be more specific about what I need to improve. If your goal is to become a better spouse, what would make you better? What are some things you could do or not do to make you a better spouse? These answers give you more specific goals. For example, I might say instead, "I want to read the Bible regularly," or "I want to stop losing my temper."

Goals should be *measurable*. Once I have a specific goal in mind, I need to determine measurements. I must evaluate whether I have met my goal or what progress I have made. What milestones can I use? How will I keep track of my progress? Returning to our examples above, "I want to read the Bible all the way through, and I do not want to raise my voice or resort to name-calling." When I have read the entire Bible, I have met my goal. At any time during the process, I can count how many books, chapters, or pages of the Bible I have read and how many remain. When I slip up and raise my voice, I perceive I am off target. My goal is now measurable!

Goals should be *attainable*. Perhaps as bad as not having a goal is having a goal I cannot meet. I cannot expect to read the entire Bible in one day, for example, or in a language I do not understand. I need to set a goal that is possible. This is not the same as setting what some call a "stretch goal." A stretch goal is when you set one goal that determines whether you were successful; then you have a higher goal that is much more difficult but can be missed without considering the effort a failure. You might look at your savings account and want to save $1,000 in one year, with a stretch goal of also paying off a credit card balance. You could be successful by saving the budgeted amount, even if you don't pay off the whole balance on the card. You met your goal. This differs from setting a goal to save $1,000 in the next three days. For most people, that would be impossible!

Goals should be *relevant*. One often-overlooked dimension to a goal is whether the goal fits its purpose. For example, my overall desire might be to become a better Christian. If so, learning Russian probably will not help me achieve my purpose. However, if my goal is to become a minister in Arkhangelsk, learning Russian would be a helpful goal to set. Sometimes disregarding the relevance of your goals is harmless—it leads to a mild distraction. But often it will sabotage your ability to reach the larger goal you believe to be more important. An example is the person who "gains the entire world but loses their soul" (Matthew 16:26).

Goals should be *timely*. Your goals need to have a time element. If your goal is to read the Bible, within what time period do you want to accomplish that goal? "I want to read the entire Bible in six months." This goal is specific, measurable, attainable (for most of us), relevant if you want to be a better Christian, and time-bound.

## WHEN ACTIONS BECOME CHARACTER

As the characteristics in Peter's *sorites* interact with one another, they combine to produce other characteristics. We have used the formation of a tornado to illustrate how all these characteristics synergize to create a powerful working faith. Since persistence corresponds to the last part of the mesocyclone, let's take a step back and view the big picture of how the first six parts fit together, lest we forget how the storm develops.

We categorize health in five classifications: physical, mental, emotional, spiritual, and social. I am amazed how many times the Bible addresses these categories. We don't even have to look further than the passage we have been studying! We began with a guiding faith supplied with diligent effort. This is the spiritual dimension. Virtue follows, which ties to your values and is emotional. Next comes knowledge, corresponding to mental health. Fourth is self-control, which is mainly physical, although it also incorporates the others too. Godliness applies the spiritual direction to the physical self-control. Then we come to a socially focused characteristic: kindness.

I don't want to jump too far ahead in our study, but we must not think of love only in terms of social behavior. Are we not told to love God with all our heart, soul, mind, and strength, and to love our neighbors as ourselves? This includes all five dimensions of health! That's why those two are the greatest commandments. They encompass all the Law and the Prophets. Therefore, love is the capstone of the *sorites*!

If you were perceptive when reading the last paragraph, you caught that I left out the one characteristic pertaining to this chapter! It was no mistake. Persistence is about taking the individual actions of faith, virtue, knowledge, etc., and turning them into a lifestyle. Persistence takes these habits to the next level—from what I *do* to what I *am*. It fuels and is fueled by the mesocyclone until culminating in an anvil-shaped cloud.

For a Christian to have the effect promised in 2 Peter 1:8-10, the corresponding causes must be present. To borrow from the imagery Jesus used, if the fruit is healthy and plentiful, the tree producing it is healthy.

Persistence is, to a great extent, morally neutral. If I do something courageous (an act of virtue) persistently, I am effective. If I do something cowardly persistently, I am useless. The same is true regarding knowledge or self-control. It's better for us to visualize persistence as a spectrum on which we measure all the other characteristics. Rather than asking, "Are you diligent and persistent?" we should measure the first characteristic by the second. Are you persistently diligent? Are you persistently worshipful, studious, self-aware, and self-controlled? The truth is, we are persistent in many things, but that persistence might be good or bad. It can either be fierce determination or stubbornness.

Eubulides, a philosopher who lived at the same time as Aristotle, was famous for writing paradoxes. One of his, the Heap Paradox, has two premises, which repeat until you reach the point of absurdity:

1) A single grain of sand is not a heap.

2) Adding a single grain of sand does not make a heap out of a non-heap.

Based on these premises, we conclude that two grains of sand do not compose a heap. We apply the second premise again, adding a grain to make three. Is it a heap now? No. So far we have no problem. However, if we get to where there are millions of grains of sand, we call that a heap. At what point did it become one? Which grain of sand did we add to make a heap? At which point do we stop referring to individual grains and instead recognize one heap?

Apply this to a man's hair—if he has a full head of hair, he is not bald. If one hair were to fall out, would we consider him bald? No. So losing one hair is not enough to make a man bald who was not so before. At the point his last hair falls out, he is bald without question. But which hair, upon falling out, made him so?

We might say the same of acts of virtue or self-control and for things we know. Does one act of valor make you virtuous? If you are not virtuous, will you become so by doing one virtuous deed? No. But somehow, over time, the habit of virtuous acts results in a virtuous person. Knowing one fact and learning one more eventually becomes great understanding. One show of self-control, added to another and then another, ultimately leads to a self-controlled life. One brick attached to one more eventually becomes a house.

Before we came to this chapter, we focused on five characteristics vital to the Christian's effectiveness. All of these are interrelated—built on top of one another. We earn no benefit if we pick and choose characteristics from the list. They are harmonious voices, each singing its part in chorus.

To think any of the other characteristics can make us productive without persistence would be delusional; however, we do it daily! If we go to the zoo and walk around for several hours, we might say, "I got my exercise in for this week!" When we use a coupon to save 50% off at our favorite boutique, we suddenly feel like budget masters. It is only by making such decisions regularly— consistently—that these things bring the desired results. Did you eat a healthy meal? Well done! Will it help you lose weight? Only if it is your regular habit. One brick does not make a house!

## STARTING TO LIVE M OW RED (REPEAT)

*"A river cuts through rock not because of its power*
*but because of its persistence."*

In Joshua 1, God told Joshua he was to take up the responsibility of leading Israel because Moses was dead. He gave him a two-part command in verse 7: "Be strong and take courage. Carefully observe all the instructions Moses my servant commanded you. Do not deviate to the right or left, so you can be successful everywhere you go."

The first part emphasizes being careful to fulfill his responsibilities. The second tells him to keep his focus where it belongs so he is not pulled away. As we noted earlier, we cannot separate persistence from any of the other habits— we must apply persistence in adopting each of the others.

This means you should measure this chapter's habit by looking at how regularly you are maintaining those from the other chapters in this book. How many days in a row have you achieved your Decide goal from chapter one? How often are you taking the time to worship or meditate? At first, I want you to pay close attention to the third point under Phase 1 below—be patient and tackle these habits slowly enough that you truly take them on.

After you have worked through this book completely and have exercised your faith to the point you can manage all the habits at once, then you can use this Repeat habit to keep track of any problem areas. Maybe one year from now, you will look over your progress and discover virtue is where you have struggled. You might reread that chapter and focus harder on it in the year to come.

## PHASE 1: CAREFULLY OBSERVE

**Stay mindful.** We are our best deceivers! As you improve at achieving your goal *automatically*, you will be tempted to let your guard down. You could slip back into bad habits at any time, so you must remain aware. In 1 Corinthians 10:12, Paul says, "Whoever thinks he stands must be careful not to fall." Once my son Jordan learned how to run, he got an enormous rush out of running with his eyes closed! He was clumsy, tried to climb everything, and always picked on his brothers who were twice his size. He fell down all the time because he was not aware of his surroundings and what he was doing!

**Keep track of your progress.** As I mentioned in the introduction, I use a habit tracker to keep up with the status of my habits. I enjoy trying to build long streaks, tallying many days in a row of maintaining a good habit or avoiding a bad one. This will not work as the *only* method of cultivating persistence, but it is a powerful tool for me. When I have a visual reminder of my habit streak, I feel an urge not to break the streak, and that helps me through moments of weakness. I would not have this tool if I were not tracking my habits daily. You might use an app, to-do list, or something else— whatever works for you. Perhaps you prefer to keep a diary about your journey. If so, be sure to read through it periodically to notice the difference in what causes you to struggle or become stronger.

**Tackle your habits patiently.** It is too tall an order to fix all the problems you find with yourself at one time. This goes back to the question of attainability. For most people, one habit at a time is the best route. Look back over your self-inventory from chapter three and pick the problem that needs the most urgent work. Then exercise the habit that helps you to overcome. Once you are at the point where it is no longer a weakness, you can continue maintaining it while starting to develop another habit. Make sure you spend enough time focused on the habit, though. If you jump to another one too soon, you will soon be fighting a war against yourself on two different fronts, and you're not likely to overcome the stubborn pressure to do what you always did in the past.

## PHASE 2: DO NOT DEVIATE

*"A goal without a plan is just a dream."*
*—Dave Ramsey*

**Expect obstacles**. Especially when you are trying to be persistent to change a habit, you cannot leave anything to your impulses. You must plan and make contingency plans for whatever obstacles come your way. For example, your healthier diet might be easy enough to maintain when everything goes according to the plan, but what happens when you take off work one day, or if relatives come to town for a surprise visit? A last-minute change can cause your old habits to steal back control of the steering wheel. While you might have done so well for months, you now risk breaking your new habit—and once you've failed once, the next failure will be much easier. Instead, you might have a few places in mind for when someone asks you to lunch, places with menu items you can eat and stay within the bounds of your diet. Similar principles apply in cases of chemical addiction: You might avoid smoking for days or even weeks, but if something changes in your routine, your impulses will rear their ugly head again. Anticipating when such obstacles might appear will allow you to plan your victory in advance. Like we talked about in Phase 1 of the Decide habit, it will be like you are stronger or faster than those who did not prepare to succeed!

**Do not accept weakness**. By this I do not mean you should be unforgiving to yourself or others. What I mean is you must not *plan* to fall short of your goal. Because you are taking potential obstacles into account, do not give yourself license to give into them! Your body produces neurochemicals that respond to most of what you do. When you give into an urge and feel satisfaction from it (whether it's eating a candy bar or paying for a stranger's lunch at the drive-through window), these neurochemicals are in play. If you plan to give into your bad habits periodically, you plan to release these neurochemicals into your body, making yourself feel rewarded for the behavior. Snickers had a series of commercials about being "hangry"—a psychological disposition caused by not having had a candy bar. The neurochemicals cause this phenomenon. If you want to short-circuit the automated behavior spurred by your nasty habits, you must not reward them by giving in periodically!

**Remember your *why*.** The habits you are trying to build are not goals themselves. They are a means to help you achieve your goal. The goal of a diet is not to "eat better" but to "feel better." In times of weakened resolve, you might convince yourself giving in is better than sticking to the diet—but will that move you toward the goal of feeling better? I'll say again what I mentioned before: Our goal with this book is not to *automate* Christianity. You cannot take something we should do with all our hearts, souls, strengths, and minds and make it automatic. But if I develop a habit that helps me stay *mindful* or gives me greater capacity to control my emotions or my body, the end goal of loving God with my all becomes possible. I am not tempted to turn to the right side or the left.

We have now come to the end of the mesocyclone section of this book. If you supplement your faith with diligence, virtue, knowledge, self-control, and persistence, you are sensing the power of your faith beginning to swell, and perhaps some firstfruits are ripening already. We are not to the goal yet—keep moving forward. So far, you have been the main one impacted. The anvil cloud has developed, but now three vital components remain that will have the greatest impact on your surroundings. There's a storm coming!

# CHASING THE STORM

-PART III-

# HOOK ECHO

# –VII–
# GODLINESS

## A COOL DOWNDRAFT

*"Every day that we're not practicing godliness, we're being
conformed to the world of ungodliness around us."*
—Jerry Bridges

AS THE NEWLY CONQUERED NATION OF ISRAEL
scattered into captivity in the late eighth century BC, the same fate loomed
over their cousins to the south. Eighty years after the fall of Samaria, a king of
Judah rose to power who would become the brightest spot in the lineage of
kings in centuries. Around 640 BC, Josiah took the throne at only eight years of
age. He grew into his role and developed a devoted respect for God's will and a
desire to do everything the right way. Around 622 BC, almost exactly a century
after the northern kingdom's demise, he launched a renovation of the temple
and funded the workers assigned to its repair.

In the process of this renovation, the priest found the "Book of the Law" in
the temple and notified Josiah. What book was this? The word used for *book*
refers to a *sefer*, or scroll (look up images of the Dead Sea Scrolls as examples).
It likely was not the whole Law of Moses (as its copies required five very large
scrolls). More likely, this is just one of those scrolls, or perhaps a fragment, since
the book had been missing.

Many parallels exist between 2 Kings 22-23 and Deuteronomy 31-32.
While we cannot know if this "Book of the Law" was Deuteronomy or a fragment

containing the last few chapters of it, the same principle applies. God repeatedly warned them in those chapters of the disaster they would face if they ever forgot God (Deuteronomy 32:15-16; 2 Kings 22:17).

Josiah enacted reforms that rid Judah of the worship of Baal, Molech, Asherah, and shrines to other Canaanite deities. He removed the priests of these shrines from their positions of influence and even sacrificed some of them at their high places (which defiled the shrines and made them unsuitable for worshiping the gods they served). He also reinstated the Passover Festival with such care that "they had not observed such a Passover since the days of the judges" (2 Kings 23:22). No Passover Festival in the days of Hezekiah, Solomon, or even David rivaled it!

Josiah displayed reverence for God's place of authority. He took the Word of God and acted according to the will of God. He practiced what he preached and "before him there was no king like him who turned to the Lord with his whole heart, soul, and might" (2 Kings 23:25). For Josiah, we cannot distinguish between his motive and motion. He understood where he needed to go and why, so immediately he went.


## WEATHER REPORT

*"We are the salt of the earth. We should add godly flavor*
*to people's lives via our words."*
—Jaachynma Agu


As the anvil cloud forms and the mesocyclone continues to rotate, the warm air at the lower level rises quickly, while the colder air makes its way down to the ground. All the turbulence swirling overhead, beyond the reach of most of the world, makes itself known in sharp downward gusts of air both in front of and behind the mesocyclone. The temperature changes rapidly. You can feel the barometric pressure drop as the upward spiral continues to pull warm air upward. It is happening.

When Jesus gave his disciples a template for prayer in Matthew 6:10, he included a line illustrating the point of godliness: "May your will be done on earth as in heaven." I said earlier, in chapter three, that when I began my work in ministry, I thought my goal was to make Christian philosophers out of the congregation. This mindset misses the point of our faith!

Jesus did not come to teach and train the saved but "to seek and save" the lost (Luke 19:10). If my faith—grounded though it might be in sound doctrines—does not reach out to those who need strength or salvation by faith, what difference is it making? Can we consider our faith sound if it does not achieve its purpose? Godliness is how we put our money where our mouth is—where philosophy becomes philanthropy and virtue becomes reality.

Having the answer to all the Bible trivia is not enough—including where you can find all the verses for a Bible study. That would be like the man given one talent by his master in Matthew 25:14-30. He could pinpoint where to find his master's money, but he did not put his master's will into action. In this parable, Jesus is the master who entrusted a deposit to his servants before going on a journey. We are the servants who received a deposit from the master, and we will give an account of our deposit at the Judgment. The question is, which servant are we?

This deposit multiplies and is returned to the Lord at Judgment, so it is not material—the material world will be dissolved on that day! It is the message of salvation. He deposited it with us on the day we believed. This message is involved in all our transactions in the world. Over time, it has the potential to grow and spread into multiple deposits in multiple people's accounts as they, too, accept and obey the faith.

Paul used similar figurative language in his letters to Timothy (1 Timothy 6:20; 2 Timothy 1:12, 14) to describe a deposit that must be protected both by God and the human entrusted with it. With this concept in mind, let us examine this servant who protected the deposit.

The man entrusted with one talent restored it in full, not losing a penny of his master's money. What was his outcome? In Matthew 25:26-27, the master responds, "You evil, procrastinating servant! So you knew I reap where I have not sown and gather where I have not scattered seed? You should have deposited my money with the bankers so I could receive my money back with interest!" This servant had everything he needed (like we have everything needed for a godly life), and he knew what the master wanted, but he did not do his will. When we accept the message without using it in our day-to-day transactions, we are like him. There is no such thing as a godly hypocrite.

## WHO'S THE BOSS?

When we use the term godly, we sometimes misunderstand it as an adverb referring to doing things the way God would—like happily refers to something done in a happy way. However, godly is an adjective that does not refer to God at all. We might as well use terms like *respectful* or *devoted*. The New Testament uses this word regarding our relationship to God, but the first-century Greeks also used it to discuss relationships to one's civil leaders and parents.

Its meaning involves deferring to someone. We are to abide by our local laws, as commanded in Romans 13 and 1 Peter 2, out of respect for God's authority, which he gave to those government leaders who (in Paul's words) "carry the sword." I might think a higher speed is safe for driving, but out of respect for the authority of those who set speed limits, I must abide by them. A teenager might have no issues staying out until early morning, but if their parents set a curfew for them, they must abide by the will of their parents. Out of respect, we take a step back.

Imagine Moses' response as he hid his face when the voice from the burning bush spoke to him. He stepped back at once and did as the voice said, removing his shoes and averting his eyes. This is the opposite of what the procrastinating servant did in Jesus' parable. He was aware his master was difficult, but that did not make him step back from what he wanted to do. He was comfortable looking his master in the eye, even though he had not done his master's will.

My two examples of yielding in the previous paragraph—to speed limits and to parental curfews—were purposely amoral. Driving thirty-six miles per hour is neither good nor bad, but if the speed limit is twenty-five, driving thirty-six becomes immoral, an infraction of the law. A teenager might have nothing but good intentions while staying out until 2 a.m., but if their curfew was 10 p.m., that is reason enough for them to be home. Arguing with authority figures shows a disregard for their authority, and even if we feel comfortable approaching our Master in worship after disregarding the law or our parents, remember they received their authority from God! Willful disobedience of their authority—which is God's authority—shows a character fault in me that I must confess and conquer if I want to be an effective Christian.

We place perhaps too much weight on the fear associated with godliness. This is because the word *fear* had a broader range of meaning in the 1600s when the King James Version was first published. So we became accustomed to seeing *fear* and walking its meaning down to respect.

Plutarch, a prolific writer of the first century AD, distinguished between the word used for godliness and another word for superstition, which referred more to fear that the pagan gods would hurt us if we did not abide by their rules. Godliness had a positive motivation—the desire to please an authority figure, whether a parent, government official, or the supreme being of their belief system.[1]

Sophocles shows this distinction in his fourth century play *Ajax*. At line 1350, Odysseus tries to convince King Agamemnon to allow an enemy soldier burial rites. Odysseus appeals to reason and what everyone believes is right, until Agamemnon stops him and says, "Godliness does not come easily to a tyrant." Because of his absolute power, he didn't care what others thought was respectful, and he had no one to please but himself.

Before you dismiss my examples of speeding and breaking curfew as petty, study with me through 1 Peter. In 2:11-12 he says, "Dear friends, I beg you to avoid bodily desires, acting like visitors and those on long journeys do, because these [desires] wage war against the soul. Keep your conduct good among the pagans so that even when they have slandered you like you were evildoers, they will glorify God on the day He intervenes, because of your good actions." Lest we interpret such a general statement the way we would like to, Peter specifies, "Submit to every human institution because of the Lord" (2:13).

What is exempt from this? Surely he doesn't mean the pagan Caesars and governors who persecuted Christianity! He continues, "whether to the emperor as the supreme leader, or to governors as entities he has sent to enforce justice on evildoers and to praise those who do what is good" (2:13-14). What if they want to hurt you? "Household servants: subject yourselves with complete reverence

---

[1] Plutarch, The Life of Numa 22.

to your masters—not only to the good and reasonable ones but also to the crooked ones" (2:18). Peter says in 2:17 that there is an underlying cause for our obedience: "Honor everyone—love the brotherhood, revere God, and honor the emperor." The way he words this sentence, "honor" acts a bookend; it is the point of the entire sentence.

Since the paragraph begins with "subject yourself to the emperor" and ends with "honor the emperor," what is the point of the whole paragraph? In context, the reason he brings up the brotherhood and God in verse 17 is that our love and respect for those two depend on our honor shown to our civil leaders!

If my disrespect to society causes the church's reputation to suffer, how am I loving the brotherhood? If I defy God's command to subject myself to human authorities, how am I respecting God? If God says to obey your parents and you refuse, are you disobeying your parents or God? So even if I don't consider breaking my curfew to be a heinous offense, my attitude toward my parents indicates my attitude toward God lacks reverence.

That is the problem. This world can sense hypocrisy and will use our hypocrisy as an excuse to refuse Jesus. If the hypocrisy they call out is ours, how do we expect to escape God's judgment? It is for such hypocrisy that many among us are fruitless in faith!

Before we leave 1 Peter 2, I want us to understand something else he is saying. He does not mean we should blindly do what these authorities ask us to do. That is not a requirement of subjecting ourselves to these powers. His point is that if we are going to disobey, it better be because God has told us to do differently and not just because we don't think the law makes sense.


## AN ATTITUDE EXPRESSED BY ACTIONS

Much debate in the religious world centers on whether salvation comes by faith or because of action. To be adamant about either is to be ignorant of both. Arguments pile up to support both sides:

"The only place in the Bible mentioning 'faith alone' says we are justified by works" (James 2:24).

"Yes, but Paul says we are saved 'by grace, through faith ... not by works, so no one can boast'" (Ephesians 2:8-9).

In each statement, we must review the contexts! Paul is arguing against the notion that one's actions—specifically the Law of Moses—can save one without Christ. Review his explanation of the dividing wall in Ephesians 2:11-18. James, meanwhile, argues against the possibility of faith existing apart from action. To say either faith or works is unnecessary is to disagree with both writers! They argue salvation requires both faith and action.

Paul devoted most of Ephesians 4-6 to explaining what Christians must do to live worthy of their calling. "So this is what I am saying and confirming in the Lord: You must not live like the pagans live any more—in the futility of their thoughts" (Ephesians 4:17). Our goal is to bear fruit, and futility of thought is the opposite! Starting with that statement, Paul used more than three dozen active imperative verbs (commands) from 4:25-6:10! His concern was on more than "faith alone." In fact, he says we were created "for good works" so that we could "walk in them" (2:10). Action is nothing without faith.

Similarly, the whole point of James' letter is we must couple faith with action, but where does it begin? "He must ask with faith, not hesitating at all, because the one who hesitates is like a wave of the sea, driven by the wind and tossed back and forth. Such a man should not expect to receive anything from the Lord" (1:6-7).

Yes, these actions are necessary, but unless they begin with faith, they are of no use. When we do not act, we abandon faith because its purpose is to affect its enviroment. "It is a sin for someone to know to do a good thing and not do it" (James 4:17). Even though he said justification is "not by faith alone," he never says faith is inherently useless. Faith is useless without action. This does not contradict Paul!

You might wonder why we are addressing the debate on faith and works in a chapter on godliness. Godliness is what we do because of what we believe. Some verses encapsulate this meaning even when they do not use the term godliness. "So since we know the terror of the Lord, we persuade people" (2 Corinthians 5:11). In other cases, the word is used: "So since these things will be destroyed, what sort of people should you be with holy behavior and godliness as you await and anticipate the arrival of the day of God?" (2 Peter 3:11-12).

## YOUR WILL BE DONE ON EARTH AS IT IS IN HEAVEN

*"I go out into America, and I am literally navigating a
minefield. Godliness has become abnormal."*
—Si Robertson

Thus far in implementing the list of characteristics in 2 Peter 1, we have mostly affected ourselves and our relationship to God. Sure, some habits work their way outward when we express them—we learn so we can teach others, and we worship so we can encourage others—but godliness is inherently rooted in our connection to the Father and brings that connection into contact with the world. It does not say the message; it displays it like a tree displaying fruit. Godliness announces unequivocally, "This is what doing God's will looks like." What virtue is toward ourselves, godliness is toward God.

Saving the lost is like the rescue of a person adrift in the sea. The helicopter hovers overhead, and a rescuer descends to the person in danger. The rescuer connects a harness to them, hoists them into the helicopter, and flies them back to dry land. When they step out of the helicopter, a crowd of witnesses breaks into celebration.

The role of godliness in this rescue is in connecting.

The goal is for the endangered person to be safe on the shore again. This requires several connections. The rescuer *connects* their harness to the helicopter so they can be safe as they approach the person in danger. Then they *fasten* another harness—which they also previously *attached* to the same helicopter—to the person in danger, to provide immediate security. Once the helicopter again *touches* the ground, both the rescuer and the one rescued *detach* from the helicopter because they have made their own *connection* to the ground. Only then does the celebration ensue.

Reaching those who are lost in sin is similar. Jesus left the ultimate place of safety to seek and save the lost—grace. Those who attach to Jesus (by faith) are able to reach out to those adrift in sin and help them become connected to Jesus by a faith of their own. The act of leaving the helicopter to reach those who are outside—giving them something concrete to allow their faith to connect back to Jesus—is godliness. Then, when the ultimate salvation comes at Jesus' return, we land safely on God's shore. We are greeted by him, and celebration commences in heaven.

Without godliness, my faith is only between me and Jesus. It reaches no one. It never makes a difference for those who need it most. This indicates either I do not believe in its importance or I do not trust my connection to the Savior, much like the servant entrusted with one talent's worth of money. This betrays a lack of faith.

Jesus followed the Parable of the Talents with the Parable of the Sheep and Goats in Matthew 25:31-46. He delivered that parable to illustrate his attitude toward those who refuse to take God's will and put it into action on the earth. "I was hungry, and you gave me nothing to eat. I was thirsty, and you gave me nothing to drink. I was a stranger, and you did not take me in; naked, and you did not clothe me; sick and imprisoned, and you did not visit me." When they challenged his rebuke, he explains, "To the same degree you did not do this for the least significant of these people, you did not do it for me."

On Christmas Eve in 2015, the cold downdraft enveloped my family when dozens of Christians acted on God's will and brought His compassion to us. We had no reason to question God's presence because His people were ever present. They loved us with his love. They fed us, gave us something to drink, clothed us, took us in, and visited us. Their diligence moved us into a new home in two days. Their faith groaned with us in worship, longing for the "land of an unclouded sky."

If I feel that the person who is lost or in need will make it without me, or it is not safe for me to go, I will not go—and if that were all, it would be bad enough. It's selfish. But when we consider God has commanded us to take the saving Message to the world, our refusal is nothing short of disobeying a direct order. We might disguise this as fear or hesitation, but we have ignored God's authority. We have abandoned those lost ones in need of rescue, and our apathy convinces them that God does not care any more than we do.

In Hebrews 12, the author of the letter corrects a gross misunderstanding about worship to God. "You have not come to a place that can be touched." He describes it as a burning fire with smoke and darkness (18). He describes the sound like a trumpet and a roaring voice, "which, when they heard it, they begged for it not to speak to them again" (19).

He is referring to the incident we can read about in Exodus 19, when Israel arrived at Mount Sinai after leaving Egypt. As God appeared to them in those terrifying manifestations, they begged him to excuse them and just talk with Moses. They preferred Moses to tell them what to do.

The author of Hebrews then says, "No, you have approached Mount Zion and the city of the living God—the heavenly Jerusalem and tens of thousands of angels arrayed majestically" (22). Others mentioned in the audience are the church of the firstborn, God (the judge of all), and Jesus, the mediator of the new covenant (23-24). What is the point of mentioning this audience? "Make sure you do not beg to be excused from the one who speaks" (25). In other words, don't tell God not to tell you what to do!

He concludes, "Through [the grace that gave us the unshakable kingdom], we must worship God in a way that pleases him, with reverence and awe, because our God is a consuming fire." This reverence, though it is not the same word translated *godliness*, expresses the same idea. It is the fusion of knowing God's will and making it happen where we are.

When I refuse to do what God commands, I am daring the Father to punish me. Paul's warning to the Romans applies to me, too: "Is that what you think— you who pass judgment on those who do these things while you practice the same things—that you will escape God's judgment? Or do you think nothing of the wealth of his goodness, tolerance, and patience, unaware that God's goodness should lead you to repentance?" (Romans 2:3-4).

Josiah had the sense to know God meant what he had said in the Law, and he responded accordingly. The king of Nineveh in Jonah 3:6-8 did the same. The Corinthians did the same, as well (2 Corinthians 7:9-11). However, the man who had one talent of money became afraid and did not act, despite what he knew of his master's expectations—like the demons who believe in God, and all they can do is tremble (James 2:19).

What about you? You know what God wants from us—what he expects in terms of our holiness and diligence. The one-talent question is whether you will do anything about it!

# Starting to Live MPOW RED (Practice)

*"Sin grows when we think we deserve something from God.
Godliness grows when we remember we are debtors to God."*
—*Timothy Keller*

## Phase 1: Enact God's Will

**Pray for your authorities.** Paul commands us to pray for our civil leaders in 1 Timothy 2:2, and we should, but they are not the only ones. In Hebrews 13:17 the author says, "Pray for your leaders and respond willingly to them because they stay awake watching over your souls as they will have to give an account. Do that so they can do it joyfully and not complaining, because that would be of no benefit to you." Some take this to refer to church leaders, and I agree, but it does not specify church leaders—just leaders. Go back to my petty example of breaking curfew earlier in this chapter. I know when I came in late as a teenager, my parents lost sleep watching for me. It was very much in my hands whether I would make their job enjoyable or burdensome, and that would affect me in return. I must confess I often gave them reason to complain on late nights like those! The same goes for law enforcement. If you get a ticket, before you complain they should be out there picking up someone who is committing an actual crime, remember they would have the time to do that if they did not have to write tickets to people who refuse to obey the simplest kind of law! Pray for them. Pray for anyone in charge of your life, whether in a civil, physical, or spiritual capacity. They need it.

**Prioritize the mystery of godliness.** Think back to a day when you truly felt greatness and possibility throughout the day. I can think of several—my first "real job;" when I went off to college and walked around feeling like a proper adult for the first time; my wedding day; and the days when each of my children were born.

Did you have a feeling you needed to slow down and soak it all in, knowing this was a big deal? Looking back, I can remember several days at my first job wondering when I would have a better one, and I remember those days in college just waiting for the semester to end. There are days when I completely miss how blessed I have been with my marriage and my children, and I focus instead on the tedious drudgery. Go to work; come home tired to a loud house, where every minute is hectic and everyone is tired; go to bed; wake up early; repeat several times; get paid; pay bills; start over. In my case, I have a terrific job. I have the best family. I just forget sometimes because I do not re-center my focus. Paul told Timothy the mystery of godliness was great, and then he laid that mystery out in sentences that are just right for us to cheer them. Jesus came in the flesh! He was proven by the Spirit! He was seen by angels! He was proclaimed to all nations! He was believed in the world! He was taken up into heaven! The next time you feel like your life doesn't mean very much, remember you get to share this mystery of godliness with the world!

**Do not neglect your gifts.** On one hand, we have the servant entrusted with one talent's weight of money. Because of his fear and mistrust of his abilities, he hid and neglected the money until his master returned. On the other, we have Paul explicitly telling Timothy not to neglect his gifts in 1 Timothy 4:14. Paul describes Timothy's gift as miraculous—he received it when the elders laid their hands on him. However, this command applies just as well to the non-miraculous gifts we have. We need to discover our gifts first, and then we need to work to develop them. Paul said, "Devote yourself to these and persist in them so your progress may be obvious to everyone" (4:15). Sadly, we do this backward. If a student in high school discovers good grades come without much effort, how hard will they study? How many honor roll high school graduates do you know whose GPA bottomed out in their freshman year of college? How many star athletes in middle school end up average athletes in high school? If you want to be effective, you must practice. Someone who makes a habit of practicing and has little talent will beat someone who has talent and little practice. Now imagine what happens when you have ability *and* practice! There are things you are better qualified to do than others—find those things and develop them, and let them be tools to help you be productive in faith.

## PHASE 2: EXEMPLIFY GOD'S WILL

**To those who are of the faith.** If you read 1 Timothy 4:12 in various translations, you will find some ambiguity in Paul's command for Timothy to be an example. Is he to be an example to the believers or an example of the believers to those who were outside the faith? Based on Paul's practices elsewhere, like in Romans 1:17,[2] he could be mindful of both points and wording his sentence in a way that gives it a fuller meaning. The context of the letter (church members should strive for true doctrine) indicates to me that if it is one or the other, Paul wanted Timothy to be an example to the believers. Paul describes the areas of life where Timothy should exemplify godly behavior. Use these to test the caliber of the example you set. What does the quality of your speech illustrate to other Christians? Using the self-inventory habit from our chapter on virtue, probe deeply into the example set by your conduct, purity, and displays of love and faith. When people picture the model Christian's conduct, and they think of you, your effectiveness and influence over them is much greater. This is especially true if you are in a leadership role—whether you are an elder, deacon, minister, teacher, or point person for a community outreach program.

---

[1] For a description of Paul's purposeful ambiguity, see page 48 of Dunn, James D. G. Romans 1-8. Vol. 38A. Word Biblical Commentary. Dallas: Word, Incorporated, 1988.

**To those who are outside the faith.** Even if Paul did not mean "Be an example of the believers," Peter's comments in 1 Peter 2-3 make that directive more than plain. A careful reader will find much in common among 1 Peter 2:18-3:7, Colossians 3:18-4:1, and Ephesians 5:22-6:9. All three explore relationship dynamics between husbands and wives, parents and children, and masters and servants. Have you ever wondered why? Aristotle also talked about these three pairs of roles in *Politics*. This was the basic structure of the Greek household in antiquity! Apparently (according to 1 Corinthians 14:38 and other passages) early Christians decided they should break free of human authority because Christ was now their king. Servants called masters *brother*, and husbands and wives called one another *brother* or *sister*. Many people in the traditional Greek world viewed this as inappropriate—tearing the fabric of society. This was the subject of many early criticisms of Christianity by those who did not believe, and perhaps because of this, the New Testament authors addressed it multiple times. Yes, we are now under Christ and not Caesar—but we still need to be good citizens! Paul told Timothy, "all who want to live a godly life by Christ Jesus will suffer persecution" (2 Timothy 3:12). What sense would there be in me giving them just cause for their mistreatment of me? As you strive to practice your faith, focus on being a good citizen. Be mindful of the criticisms launched against believers, and do not add unnecessary fuel to the fire. By "honoring the emperor" you show respect for God and love to your Christian family (1 Peter 2:17).

**To those who are closest to you.** Jesus said in the Sermon on the Mount we have a tendency to ignore what is right in front of us as we try to correct what is wrong in the world. "You hypocrite! First get the log out of your own eye; then you will see well enough to remove the sawdust from your brother's eye" (Matthew 7:5). Did you know this is also true of our relationships? Have you ever heard someone try to tell another person they are raising their children incorrectly? Have you seen people do it when their own family is a wreck? If you will permit me, I want to adapt one of Jesus' statements to make a point. What does it benefit someone to convert the entire world but lose their family? What would someone give up to save their family? Despite common sense, many of us overlook the need to set an example for our families. Men, how will your children understand their heavenly Father's love for them if they do not observe it in their earthly father? Parents, if you want your children to trust God, they must be able to trust you and see you trusting God too—not "losing your religion" because you will not control your temper or because you did not have faith. Monkey see, monkey do, and Christian see, Christian do. If you want to have an impact on your family's faithfulness, there is no shortcut—put God's will into action and exemplify it in front of them. Let them witness your good works and glorify God! (Matthew 5:16). Or if there are some character flaws in your life that need work, let your family watch you work to correct them. Seeing an unsavable soul saved brings glory to God! (Galatians 1:23-24).

# –VIII–

# KINDNESS

## THE RAIN BEGINS TO FALL

*"Every kid is one caring adult away*
*from being a success story."*
—Josh Shipp

I 'VE NEVER SEEN ANYTHING LIKE IT," THE HOTEL manager says, adjusting the "Ring for Service" sign at his front desk. "I thought I understood people until the night that Samaritan came in here.

"He brought some guy with him, and let me tell you—someone had put him through the wringer! He could barely get around; we pretty much had to carry him to his room. The Samaritan had given him first aid, but he wanted to be sure he had a safe place to sleep and recover.

"In the morning, the Samaritan gave me a bag of money and said to let the guy stay there a few days. He said, 'If it's not enough, I'll settle up when I come back.'

"I mean, in this neighborhood I've seen some beatings. I've taken care of some fellows in terrible shape. I've never seen kindness like that—from a Samaritan, no less. It was news to me for sure."

We'll come back to this story of kindness, but first, imagine someone who overcame cruel treatment from his classmates because of his weight. He struggled with anger and self-esteem issues but controlled himself so well, most would never suspect it. This boy grew up to be a minister who would do much of his private study in the original languages of the Bible, Hebrew and Greek. He had the discipline to wake up around 5 a.m. every morning, swim a mile, and keep his body weight at 143 pounds for much of his adult life—the number being a tribute to the words "I love you" having one, four, and three letters, respectively.

Could you believe such a person would exist—a person who valued self-control, diligence, knowledge, virtue, and faith to such a high degree? I am telling you he did, and his name was Fred Rogers.

Like many Americans born in the latter half of the 20th century, I grew up watching Mister Rogers' Neighborhood, but I didn't understand at the time the social impact Fred Rogers was making with his show.

In 2018 I watched a documentary called *Won't You Be My Neighbor?* I highly recommend it! The documentarian went to see who the real Fred Rogers was, to find out whether he was anything like his character on the show. I worried at first that I would learn something that would color my perception of him because so many despicable secrets had become public for other heroes of family television. I didn't want to see another one ruined!

However, in the words of the documentary, "He's not only who he is on television, he's actually even better in real life."

For example, Rogers was on the phone talking with a man who was skeptical of him when he asked, "Do you know what is the most important thing in the world to me right now? Having this conversation with [the name of the person talking to him]."

He didn't say *you*—he said their name.

Whether we observed him on the show or in person, what seemed to grab our attention more than anything else was Mister Rogers' kindness. He was always encouraging and complimenting the people he met. He cooled his heels in a little pool with a person of color on public television—in 1968—and then toweled off his new friend's feet when they were finished. He spoke with a boy named Jeff Erlanger who was in an electric wheelchair and sang, "It's you I like and not your fancy chair," emphasizing people-first language about a decade before psychologists advocated it. Jeff was not a "disabled person"—he was a boy, foremost, who had a "fancy chair."

If you doubt the impact kindness can have on the world—or the impact any of those characteristics listed in 2 Peter 1:5-7 can have—Fred Rogers is Exhibit A.

## WEATHER REPORT

*"Based on what I see, brotherly love is as scarce in our time*
*as brotherly hatred was among men of old."*
*—Plutarch*

A tornado warning has been issued. Radar can detect the rotation in the atmosphere formed by the mesocyclone of virtue, knowledge, and self-control that spins persistently. The cold front of diligence continually meets the warm updraft of faith, finally causing a stiff, cool downdraft to reach the ground—the Father's will is being done on earth as it is in heaven.

The next telltale sign is precipitation. Hard rain and hail cover the earth, radar depicting their presence in regions of dark red in front of and behind the mesocyclone.

You might have heard meteorologists talk about a hook echo. This is the spinning area with little precipitation almost surrounded by heavy precipitation. The funnel might or might not be touching the ground, but radar indicates a tornado is forming.

At least twice, the New Testament links precipitation to uncharacteristic kindness. In Matthew 5:43-45, Jesus corrects his audience's perception of the "royal law"—loving your neighbor as yourself. They had become accustomed to believing this meant they should love only their neighbors, allowing them to treat foreigners and enemies with less respect. Jesus told them to love their enemies and pray for those who persecuted them so they might be their heavenly Father's children since he "causes rain to fall on the just and unjust."

In the ancient Hebrew's mind, being a "son of" anything was to live up to its reputation. For example, a "son of thunder," as Jesus called James and John in Mark 3:17, would have had a loud, terrifying personality. A "son of man," as God called Ezekiel and Jesus called himself, emphasizes the humanity of the person being addressed. Being a "son of your Father who is in heaven" in Matthew 5:45

means you live up to the Father's reputation. And what did he say the Father does? He allows life-giving rain to fall on those who deserve it and on those who don't. To be kind to the undeserving is to be perfect like He is perfect (48).

In Romans 12:20-21, Paul shares how to treat our enemies: "If your enemy is hungry, feed them. If they are thirsty, give them a drink. By doing this you are piling up burning coals on their head. Do not be conquered by evil—conquer evil with good."

This verse is the conclusion to a long section of simple instructions (simple in the sense of brief sentences—not necessarily easy to follow!). He begins in verse 9: "Love must be without hypocrisy." All the commands from 9-21 play supportive roles to the context. Because we will address general Christian love in the next chapter, for now let's focus on the sections that pertain to kindness.

In verse 10, Paul says: "Be devoted to one another with brotherly love." This is represented in Peter's list by the word kindness.

To this point in our study, we have examined several terms the Greco-Roman philosophers analyzed. Brotherly love is not one of them! Before the New Testament era, they used this term only regarding the affection and care shown for one's physical family. When Plutarch wrote the statement from the beginning of this section in his discourse "On Brotherly Love," he used a famous set of conjoined twins from Greek mythology to prove the scarcity of brotherly love.[1] "To use a father's wealth, friends, and slaves together is as unbelievable and amazing as for one soul to make use of the hands, feet, and eyes of two bodies." Even in the 21st century, sadly, the death of a parent often brings about the death of relationships between brothers and sisters. It becomes a race to "get mine" before my siblings do!

In 4 Maccabees 13:19-27,[2] brotherly love is portrayed as a gift from God cultivated by shared experience—they were gestated in the same womb (20), nursed at the same fountains (21), and grew under the same education of God's law and family values (22-24). So Jews living in the period between Malachi and Matthew restricted brotherly love to family.

That would change when a new Teacher arose in Galilee.

---

[1] These twins, the sons of Aktor and Molione, fought in the Trojan War according to *The Iliad*.
[2] This is an apocryphal work written around the same time as the New Testament.

## A New Commandment

This helps us to understand what was so groundbreaking about Jesus' teaching. While celebrating one last Passover Seder with the disciples, Jesus said, "I am giving you a new command—love one another. Just like I loved you, you also must love one another. By this, everyone will know you are my disciples, since you have love for one another" (John 13:34-35).

Rather than restricting this affection to my physical family, I now must treat my spiritual family as physical brothers and sisters.

And why not? Were we not all born of the same womb? When Nicodemus asked Jesus if it were possible to enter one's mother's womb a second time to be born, Jesus said, "Unless someone is born of water and the Spirit, they cannot enter God's kingdom" (John 3:5). Have we not nursed at the same fountains? Peter says, "Like newborn infants desire the pure spiritual milk, so you may grow on it" (1 Peter 2:2). Peter had already talked about the need to love one another like family in 1:22: "Since you have purified your souls by obedience to the truth resulting in sincere brotherly love, love one another deeply with a pure heart." He mentioned it again in 3:8-9: "Finally, everyone must show like-mindedness, sympathy, brotherly love, compassion, and humility. Do not repay evil with evil or abuse with abuse—instead, repay with a blessing. You were called for this purpose—so you would inherit a blessing." According to Peter, loving one another is the natural response of being purified and is a prerequisite to receiving the blessed inheritance from our common Father.

A variation of the same command appears in three of the passages we have studied: "Do not repay evil with evil" (Matthew 5:39; Romans 12:17; 1 Peter 3:9). This is a core component of the New Testament's teaching about kindness. This sets us apart, as Jesus said in Matthew 5:46-47: "If you love those who love you, what reward do you have? Even tax collectors do that, don't they? And if you greet your brothers only, what are you doing better than others? Even pagans do that, don't they?"

So we have our litmus test of brotherly love—if the way you treat people does not differ from the way unbelievers do, what makes you better? We might try to massage our consciences by saying we go to church, or we were baptized. As a counterpoint, if your attendance at worship services and your baptism have not made you any better of a person, why should your friends and neighbors follow you in doing that? Having a worldly attitude about how to treat others and who deserves your kindness will ruin your effectiveness!

Jude uses strong terms when he refers to those who fail this test. "These people are reefs at your fellowship meals. They feast with you but irreverently shepherd themselves" (Jude 12). In the first place, "reef" is a weird thing to call someone. The Greek word for *reef* is spelled almost the same as the word for *stain*, although Greek spelling was not standardized then, and the word for *stain* is spelled differently in every case I could find except for one (which was from the third century AD). The King James Version opts for that meaning, perhaps based on the similarity of the passage to 2 Peter 2:13, but each of the other descriptions in Jude 12-13 is a natural phenomenon. Furthermore, in an economy supported by sea trade, the meaning would be apparent. These false brothers were (and some today are) hidden dangers; above the surface of the water, they appear fine, but beneath the surface lurk dangers that will ruin you.

These people eat with you, but they are not with you. They assemble at those meals to feed themselves—one term used when Jesus told Peter to "feed my sheep" is the word used for them shepherding themselves. They are like the ones Paul reprimanded in 1 Corinthians 11:21; they made sure they got theirs first with the Lord's Supper, so some were drunk, and they left others hungry. These people come to worship and express a love for God and the Word, but they show no concern for their brothers and sisters in Christ.

The second description is, "They are waterless clouds carried along by the wind" (Jude 12). This uses the same language as James 1:6. "Whoever hesitates is like a wave of the sea driven by the wind and tossed around." As with faith (James' focus in that verse), if you lack brotherly love, you will treat people differently based on what is convenient. "The wind" carries you as you go with the flow, doing what comes easily. This is not the path to influence!

Even more intriguing is the concept of "waterless clouds." He is not referring to clouds made of something other than water vapor; the key point is, they bring no rain. The dark clouds gather and hover overhead as you feel the temperature change, but then nothing happens. The wind continues to blow them across the sky, and your crops receive no rain. The world sees us and says, "You were supposed to make things different!"

These are church members we welcome into the family, and we are excited about their impact on the ministry of the church, but eventually they just come and go, and no one is any better off. They are concerned only with being fed, not with feeding others. Any ministry they do is for themselves and not from a love of the brotherhood.

They are "autumn trees without fruit that are twice dead and uprooted" (Jude 12). When you pass a tree in autumn, you should be able to spot fruit—it has had all spring and summer to grow and nurture fruit, and to have none is a waste of soil and time. As a result, farmers typically cut down fruitless trees and uproot them to let the rest have better nourishment.

Death by judgment is called a "second death" in Revelation 2:11 and 20:14. These souls will have an eternal punishment, as the end of Jude 13 also says.

Now, the whole point of Peter's list of characteristics in the *sorites* is to have a faith that is "neither useless nor unproductive." Remember—before the Industrial Revolution, "productive" primarily referred to the quality of *bearing fruit*, not getting things done. This is where I believe Christians today miss the point of productive faith. We are so focused on efficiency and order, we neglect the need to bear fruit. When is it acceptable for a congregation not to grow? How did we get to the point where we need to reinterpret congregational growth as "in spirit" so we don't have to apologize for not growing "in number"? Congregations do not grow in spirit—Christians do! Congregations grow in number. If a congregation is not growing in number, its Christians are fruitless.[3] And if Christians are fruitless, they are unprepared for Judgment. This might sound extreme, but do a word search in the New Testament for fruit and read how many times fruitlessness is repaid with punishment—then tell me if I'm overreacting.

## LOVE IS A VERB, NOT A SECOND-HAND EMOTION

> *"Unexpected kindness is the most powerful, least costly, and most underrated agent of human change."*
> —*Bob Kerrey*

---

[3] An orchard is not fruitless unless its trees are fruitless.

In chapter two I mentioned that faith cannot be separated from action. For example, Hebrews 11:4 says, "By faith, Abel offered a better sacrifice." The same was true of diligence in chapter one—so many occurrences of "diligence" involved the action to perform: "Be diligent to come before winter."

Now look at how love is used in the New Testament: "God loved the world, so he gave" (John 3:16). "Love does no wrong to one's neighbor, so love is the fulfillment of the Law" (Romans 13:10).

In the previous chapter, we learned godliness was a culmination of several characteristics that manifest themselves in godly behavior (faith, diligence, virtue, knowledge, and self-control). The same is true for brotherly love. Although it is unique in its demonstration, brotherly love can only exist where those qualities are present. I can't love my sister unless I treat her with understanding. I can't love my brother unless I use self-control with him. I can't love my Father in heaven without loving those made in his image (James 3:9-10).

But to whom must I show this undeserved kindness? The expert in the Law who questioned Jesus in Luke 10 had this question. If I can prove so-and-so is not my neighbor in God's eyes, then I am excused from treating them with kindness—right?

In Matthew 12:46-50, Jesus was talking to the crowds when his mother and brothers came to speak with him. When someone told him, he said, "Whoever does the will of my Father who is in heaven—that person is my brother, sister, and mother" (50). I am going to put this bluntly, so consider this a disclaimer: If you have trouble getting along with fellow believers in Christ, this passage needs to be setting off alarm bells in your mind. Reconcile it with Matthew 5:23-24: "So if you are offering your sacrificial gift at the altar, and there you remember your brother has something against you, leave your gift there in front of the altar and first go reconcile with your brother. Then come and offer your gift." I recognize this passage is describing Jewish worship practices, but tell me— what command in the New Testament overrides this to keep it from applying to Christian worship? If you think you can worship God without resolving your differences with his people, you are mistaken. It is not as simple as finding another place to worship or running someone out of town.

Now one might say, "In that passage, the one offering the worship was in the wrong and needed to apologize. It is different if they wrong me." I ask you to look at Matthew 18:15: "If your brother sins against you, go tell him his fault—between you and him only. If he listens to you, you have regained your brother." So if you are at fault for the disagreement, who acts first? You do. If they are at fault for it, who acts first? You do. No excuses!

One might raise the counterpoint: "What if the brother doesn't listen? This passage shows us the steps we take to withdraw our fellowship—are we required to reconcile with them even then?"

Pay close attention to the verbiage. If the brother does not listen to you, take someone with you and go again. This is still you talking to the brother—just not as privately as before (18:16). This is not you talking to two or three others to get their opinion. That is gossip. Call it what you wish, but recognize what it is. When you have gone to him yourself, and have gone back with witnesses who can attest to the wrong and to his refusal to correct it, you take it to the church assembly, where the person is now asked to respond publicly. If they do not, only then do you withdraw your fellowship (verse 17). Unless you follow these directions to the letter, do not comfort yourself that you have done what is right. Instead, if you go outside these bounds and speak to others about it, you have now sinned against your brother, and Matthew 5:23-24 applies to you.

Just to be sure we cover these bases, let's read what Paul says after the church was established—so we cannot say "that was just for those under the old covenant." Paul says in 1 Corinthians 6:7-9, "It is already a total defeat for you to have lawsuits against one another. Why would you not prefer to suffer injustice instead? Why would you not prefer to be deprived [of what they try to take from you]? But no, you commit injustice yourselves and deprive them—and do this to your brothers! Do you not know those who commit injustice will not inherit God's kingdom? Do not be deceived!" Dear friend, it is simple—love your brother, and be more willing to be disadvantaged rather than take advantage, or be lost!

Now, it's difficult to let go of grievances—I don't mean to say it is easy. But as we read about the expert in the Law in Luke 10:29 "wanting to justify himself," let us give pause and make sure we are not doing the same thing. When is our love required?

In the introduction to this chapter, you read what the innkeeper in Jesus' parable might have said as he described the Good Samaritan. The innkeeper probably did not exist other than as a character in the parable, but the reaction he had was genuine.

As Jesus wove together the details of his story, he said, "By chance, a priest was traveling down that road" (Luke 10:31). Do you think the religious elite who tried to trap Jesus in his words thought this might be the hero of the story? How noble would it be for a priest to stoop down and care for a stranger—no one would expect him to treat the man like a neighbor! But he crosses the road and passes by the man.

The questioner might try to assuage his disappointment by justifying the priest—he's a busy man with important things to do. We shouldn't expect him to sink to this level.

A Levite happens by and does the same thing. Would we consider him devoid of brotherly love? Well, if the religious leaders are not responsible to care for such a person, maybe that lets me off the hook! In similar fashion, each of us could say, "If they won't do it, why should I?"

Then comes the Samaritan—someone the Jews would call a dog because of his mixed race and mixed religion. Samaritans set up their own places to worship—they wouldn't dare come to the holy temple in Jerusalem. They had distinct interpretations of the Law of Moses! The only thing that might make them neighbors of any Jew was the shared border between their nations.

Well, that and the fact this Samaritan *decided* to show kindness to a Jewish man down on his luck.

When he saw him, he felt compassion (Luke 10:33), but have we not all at some point felt compassion without showing it? He acted on his.

When Jesus finished his parable in verse 36, he asked a simple question: "Who proved to be a neighbor to the man who fell at the feet of the robbers?"

There was only one correct answer. "I suppose the one who acted with mercy for him" (37).

"Now you go do the same."

The expert in the Law, who had been trying to justify himself, was caught in his own trap. He could have argued, "Why should I?" Why would it have been his responsibility to show kindness? Instead he was left thinking, "I cannot let this Samaritan outdo me!" One act of unexpected kindness destroyed every argument of self-justification.

I mentioned Malcolm, Julie, and Megan in the introduction. They drove almost three hours to bring us a trailer full of household necessities. We didn't know them, but they had survived a tornado in 2011 that destroyed their home, and the kindness shown to them by Christians changed their lives. They decided to pay that kindness forward to my family when they heard about us on Facebook.

To this day, what they did reminds me that my neighbor does not have to live in my neighborhood—or even my state. My neighbor might wear the wrong colors on game day—they might even speak a different language. They have done nothing to earn my kindness, but that cannot be my excuse. They are not the reason I am to be kind. You see, Jesus showed the same compassion for me when I was worthless and unlovable, and it is my turn to pay it forward. Don't do what people deserve or what they expect; do what Jesus would do. You call yourself a child of God. Prove it.

## Starting to Live EMPOW RED (Encourage)

*"Try to be a rainbow in someone else's cloud."*
—*Maya Angelou*

### Phase 1: Be good to Yourself

**Recognize what you need.** The Royal Law requires you to love your neighbor "as yourself." So before you can love your Christian family properly, you must love yourself properly. Encouraging others causes you to expend courage. If you spend your energy and time building up others without giving attention to yourself, you will burn out. Look at the example of Jesus. In Matthew 14, we read of the execution of John the Baptist. His disciples went to tell Jesus. What was his first response? He went to be alone. Unfortunately, the people heard where he was and went to find him. He ended up teaching them for much of the day and fed them (this was when he fed 5,000 with a few pieces of bread and fish). What happened next? He sent the disciples by boat to the other shore of the sea of Galilee as he dismissed the crowd (22). Once he did that, he ascended the mountain alone to pray. If any passage shows me the humanity of Jesus in response to the demands of ministry, it is this one. What he needed was to spend time processing his grief for John and praying, but he first had to take care of the crowd and what they needed. However, he still took time for himself. Rather than getting on the boat with his disciples and lamenting the lack of "me time," he *made* time for what he needed. I can still prioritize self-care despite the demands life places on me. Before you can love others, recognize what you need and provide it.

**Affirm yourself.** If you have put in the work leading up to this chapter, you have developed a virtuous and godly outlook guided by faith. You have gained control of yourself with diligence and persistence and have sought knowledge of what you should do. Because of that, you should now be confident you are on the right track. However, self-doubt is a paralyzing possibility, despite your best preparation. One way to renew your courage is to take your personal moral inventory from chapter three and declare out loud to yourself that you will continue to do the good things from your inventory and will refuse to give in to your vices. Make this promise to yourself each morning and give yourself recognition when you make progress. For example, if your temper was one fault, resolve not to lose your temper today—and allow yourself no excuse to do so. Each morning, say, "I have done better with my temper and have not lost control in [however many] days." This self-affirmation will eventually supplement your motivation and help you be persistent. Further, you will have a constant reminder of both your responsibility and progress. When someone notices the change in your character, you can tell them how hard the struggle was before and how many days since you last gave in. Even if you slip back into it at some point, remind yourself of the long periods of success and be kind to yourself. You have made tremendous progress!

**Understand the value of Jesus' blood.** As we deal with our vices and temptations, it is especially challenging to maintain a loving attitude toward ourselves. No one knows how difficult it is to overcome your temptations more than you do—others might think you are not trying, or you don't have it so tough. You know the truth. You are aware how easy it is to slip back into old habits. You remember how many times you failed to keep that promise to yourself to be better. You might think it's not worth it—you are too far gone. That is when you need to remind yourself of your value. Value comes in many forms. Some of it is bestowed by someone else—like an heirloom that is only valuable to those who loved the original owner. Some value is intrinsic, as it is with money. What you value is demonstrated by what you are willing to give up or not. Your soul is valuable to God, and his willingness to trade his Son's life for it proved this, even when we were his enemies and without strength (Romans 5:8-10). The question, then, is whether you will value your soul as much as God does. Is it more valuable to you than avoiding the struggle to overcome temptation? If my temptation—that unhealthy habit—is beyond my control, it's embarrassing to admit it. It can be humiliating. It can even be financially costly—but is that cost anywhere near the value of my soul?

## PHASE 2: BE A GOOD NEIGHBOR

**Recognize what they need.** Earlier in this chapter, we noted the litmus test of brotherly love, which is how you treat those who do not deserve kindness. Mature faith supplemented by brotherly love is as effective and world-changing as worldly prejudice is ineffective. When we examined self-control, one tip for developing the Overcome habit was to recognize the triggers that pressure us into bad habits. Armed with this knowledge, can you see what others need despite what they deserve? If your child is in a terrible mood and displaying defiant behavior, is it because they lack discipline and do not care about you, or are they struggling with something and don't know how to cope or ask for help? If you recognize the need and give your support instead of punishment, you not only help them trust you enough to come to you in the future, you also spare them from the added strain you would have piled on top of their struggle! If you treat people the way they deserve to be treated, you have become a waterless cloud, promising rain but unable to deliver. You were called to be different and make a difference, but you are just like everyone else. If you want to be different, you have to do what no one else is willing to do.

**Do not punish good deeds.** Whenever someone makes a much-needed moral decision that took a long time and lots of encouragement from others, it is tempting for those encouragers to express frustration. When your daughter cleans her room without being asked, you might want to say, "It's about time! Did you find any rodents living in there?" When your son comes home before curfew, you might say, "What, was everything closed?" Please do not do this! Human behavior is not simple, and I'm not an expert in it, but are these kinds of comments constructive or destructive? Tell me this—if you feel you will receive sarcasm for doing what someone wants and mild frustration if you don't, what are you more likely to do? Chances are it will be whatever is the easy thing. How often is that the right choice? Criticizing someone when they have done the right thing will make it less likely for the improvement to continue. This is a common problem for many of us—with our spouses, children, friends, and co-workers. One of the worst times is when we do this to new or returning Christians! "I have been wondering when you would come back to church!" Take this seriously—if they should know better, chances are they do. Imagine the struggling Christian who wants to resume attending worship, but they dread these conversations with everyone. Blame them if you wish, but if your comments so much as made it easier for someone not to come to worship, don't give them all the blame. Praise good deeds; do not punish them.

**Value them.** What is the difference between encouragement and manipulation? Value. If you treat people a certain way so they will do something for you, you are valuing yourself. In this case, they are the currency—you are spending your relationship with the person to purchase a better outcome for yourself. This is manipulation. On the other hand, if you are spending yourself to invest in them, you are valuing them. This was what proved Fred Rogers was more than a character on a TV show. He invested in people. In each of his interactions with people, he gave them the most important slot on his schedule—the present moment. I've said it before, but there is never a more important time than right now. When you have the diligence and self-control to be present with people—100 percent present—you show them their value. This is especially important when you are unsure how to help someone. What should you do? Be present. Call them, visit them, and expect nothing from them. By that, I mean don't expect them to respond to you, thank you, or grieve in the way you think you would. When you don't know what to say, say nothing. Be there. Chances are, they wouldn't remember what you said later anyway (unless you said something that hurt them). They will remember you were present and invested in them.

# CHASING THE STORM

## –PART IV–

## FUNNEL CLOUD

# –IX–

# LOVE

*"Don't worry about other people's opinions of you.*
*God never told you to impress people, only to love them."*
—Dave Willis

H E PEERS OUT THE WINDOW AT HIS SONS IN THE field while they tend the livestock with the hired men. A smile crosses his face as he reflects on the blessings in his life. "I remember when we struggled to have enough to eat. Now God has blessed me with enough for both of my boys to feed their families!" As any father would, he loved his boys. "Sure, they can be a handful—no one's perfect. But I've tried to raise them right. I hope, with God's help, they will be great men one day."

Then everything went wrong.

It started as a simple act of defiance but escalated rapidly, ending as the father separated his assets into three equal parts—two for his firstborn (his birthright), and one for his younger son. "Where did I go wrong? Why does my little boy want my wealth more than me? And why didn't his brother step in and help me talk him out of this madness?"

The relationship worsens. He walks in on his son negotiating the price of a field with a neighbor. Then stranger after stranger shows up with money in hand before tucking a piece of property under his arm and walking away. The father thinks, "For years I worked to build something to be proud of—something my sons could be proud of. I never dreamed they would do this."

One day he wakes up to see no strangers and no neighbors—all is quiet. His older son leans in the door and swallows his frustration. "He's gone. He took his money and left while we were asleep."

In the months that followed, what thoughts must have gone through the father's mind? Think about it like this—if your children put themselves at risk because of their choices, what do you feel? Anger? Sometimes, but doesn't it come mostly from fear of what they will bring on themselves? It's not a selfish anger. You're not hoping they get what is coming to them—you hope they come to their senses!

Do you think we misunderstand God's anger at sin? Is he angry we defied him, or is he worried we are fattening ourselves for the day of slaughter? This father was hurt! As he thought about the reckless decisions his son was making— how tough he was making things on his future—it must have weighed on him every day.

Many miles away, the young man rubs his eyes and stares at his reflection in the trough water he has just poured. "Will I get to eat today? How did I end up like this?" He contemplates his options but settles reluctantly on his choice. "I need to go home." He places his hands behind his head and stretches. "What will they say? Will they say anything? Will Dad be angry? I don't think I can handle the lecture." It's almost enough to make him change his mind. "But I guess it's better than starving to death."

How differently the father and son see things! The young man keeps his focus on the past, regretting every false step he made. The father hopes for one more chance. He spends every day hoping against hope it will be today. Every night he tries to sleep and listen for his son at the same time.

One day, a figure appears in the distance, and the way he walks looks familiar. The old man's heart leaps, but his head cautions him. "What are the odds it's really him? I should wait until he's closer so I can be sure." His need for closure outmatches his patience as he gets up to go meet whoever this is. With each passing step, his speed and confidence increase. He breaks into a run as tears run down his face.

Where is his anger now? Where is the hurt? Where is the demand for restitution? They are gone—only unspeakable joy remains! "Bring nice clothes—bring a ring—bring shoes! Plan a party—we are celebrating tonight!"

It's at this point we learn the purpose of this parable, which is found in Luke 15:11-32. Its most popular name is "The Prodigal Son," but this misses a key figure in the parable. In Luke 15:1-2, we learn the context of the three parables told in the chapter. "All the tax collectors and sinners came to listen to Jesus, so both the Pharisees and scribes complained: 'This man welcomes sinners and eats with them!'"

Granted, the parables about the lost sheep and lost coin had an important point to make—there is celebration in heaven when even one sinner repents of sin (verses 7 and 10). This concept is part of the third parable, too, as the father prepares a feast to celebrate his son's return. If this were the main point of the parable, however, it would end here, like the other two did!

According to Luke's retelling, the party is going on as the older son gets home. When he finds out the celebration is to honor his good-for-nothing brother, he refuses to join in. This is when another theme of the three parables happens. In verse 4, the shepherd leaves the ninety-nine safe sheep to search for the lost one. In verse 8, the widow sets aside the coins she has and searches for the lost one. In verse 28 the father leaves the son who is "safe and sound" to find the one who refuses to come to the celebration. There's more than one way to be lost!

Talk about flipping the script! When we remember the context—that the religious elite became upset Jesus ate with sinners—we understand the father in this parable had two lost sons. One was lost because he thought nothing of his father's *legacy*. The other was lost because he thought nothing of his father's *love*.

If you have been the one who selfishly hurt your family, you remember the fear of what would happen if you tried to make amends. Will they ever trust you again? Can you do enough to earn their forgiveness? Will you spend each day in the shadow of your past, never able to belong again? That is tragic, but it could be worse. I wonder how many people have let fear prevent them from coming back to their heavenly Father. How many people tried to come back, but their "older brother" in the faith shut them out?

What if the younger son decided to come home but ran into his brother first? As his brother railed on him for the damage he had done to their father and warned him not to expect forgiveness from anyone back home, what would the younger son do? He would become distraught and give up his quest for restoration! He would go back to the streets and live out his days (however few they might be) hungry, cold, and alone. The jilted father would never again know his son—only grief. This is why it's unacceptable when we don't show the world God's love.

When the tornado destroyed my family's home in 2015, fear of weather's power was new to much of my community, but not to my family. One day when I was five years old, we took the hour-long drive to my grandparents' home in Somerville, TN. That night, a tornado passed by the house where we took shelter together. Several of my aunts, uncles, and cousins were there. I remember the electricity going on and off, and my brother, who was 18 months old, crying when the lights came on and stopping when they went off. I remember laughing—but only for a moment.

We huddled in the hallway, and my sister and some of my cousins were in the bedroom behind me. The window in that room shattered, and I heard them scream and run out into the hallway. My grandparents' bedroom was directly in front of me, and from where I sat, I could see through their window out into the front yard. Immediately after the window broke, flashing lights flew across the yard about fifty yards from the house.

I didn't know what it was at the time, but the next morning we found a significant amount of debris from my uncle's barn strewn along the tree line. To this day, I don't know if the flashing I saw was lightning, fire, or something else, but it put a healthy fear of bad weather into my mind. I came to respect the power of nature—when a tornado watch is active, we watch!

What if it had gone differently? What if my sister and cousins had stayed in the hall with us, and the door across from me had been closed? We would have heard the window break and found the debris the next morning, but I would have missed the terrifying display of power (and probably slept better at night).

God's love is no less powerful, and it is as wonderful as the storm is terrifying—but how often do we shut the door so no one witnesses His glory? How many people who needed their world turned back over were so close, but we kept them from seeing it? If only we had opened the door so they could see, we would have borne fruit. What will the Father do if he never has the chance to reconcile with them because we drove them away?

## WEATHER REPORT

---

> *"We love others best when we love God most."*
> —Kyle Idleman

Perhaps you have noticed when you try to dissolve a solid substance into a liquid that the solid begins at the bottom of the cup. For example, when you stir sugar into a glass of iced tea, it will first rest at the bottom. Imagine if you stirred the glass with the spoon relatively shallow in the tea—barely beneath the surface. How well will it dissolve the sugar? It will some, but stirring is most effective when the spoon is near the bottom of the glass, so the movement takes place nearest what you are wanting to dissolve.

The powerful characteristics described in 2 Peter 1:5-7 work this way as well. If you want to impact the lost people around you, your stirring must be as close as possible to them. If you possess a diligent, fervent faith, you might win some souls to obey the gospel. If you act with virtue, grow in knowledge, and gain control over your impulses, non-Christians will recognize you occasionally. We admit this when we say things like, "You might be the only Bible some people ever read." But how do we get the spoon to reach the bottom of the glass? How do we take the mesocyclone—that rotation in the atmosphere—and cause it to touch down? The touchdown is where the power happens.

If you get nothing else out of this book, I hope you get this: To develop a faith that changes people and flips the world upside down, you must master the two greatest commands. Love God with every part of your existence, and love your neighbor like yourself (Matthew 22:37-40). Without love, you only stir up the atmosphere above those lost souls. They will never experience the power of God because God is love (1 John 4:8).

In the introduction to this book I gave examples of the people who spent Christmas Eve helping us dig through rubble and clean insulation off our belongings. I talked about the money given to us and the miles driven by some of them to ensure we had what we needed. I knew several of these people before that day (not all of them, though), and I knew them to be faithful and godly. But their display of love in December 2015 was when the power of God touched down and flipped my world over. Instead of swirling over my head, it came down to my level and reached me. It woke me up to God's power and its supremacy over the power of nature.

There is a passage mentioning godliness that I did not note in chapter seven—2 Timothy 3:5. Paul says people will "have a form of godliness but deny its power." What is he talking about? Look at the verses immediately before it: "People will be *lovers* of themselves, *lovers* of money, boastful, arrogant, slanderers, rebellious against their parents, unforgiving, unholy, *heartless*, unpleasable, saboteurs, out of control, savage, not *loving* good, traitors, reckless, insolent, *lovers* of pleasure rather than *lovers* of God" (2-4). He proceeds to talk about them denying the power of godliness. I italicized each indictment against them that refers to love.

Six times in those three verses, we are told these people were without God's love. They did not love him or those made in his image, and so they were without God, despite their claim of godliness. For godliness to be present, the result must be love.

Let us return our thoughts to the older brother in the parable of "The Man with Two Lost Sons." Though he touted his faithfulness to his father, his lack of concern for his brother's safety was proof he was more like his brother than he thought.

You see, the younger brother was rebellious and entitled. He did not care what his father wanted—he wanted what belonged to him so he could do as he pleased. The older brother did not care that his father wanted to celebrate the younger brother's return—he refused to attend the party and felt entitled to a celebration with his friends, which the father had never granted to him despite his loyalty.

The father even treats them the same: "Everything I have is yours" (Luke 15:31). He does not say "Everything will be yours" (as in, after the father's death). When the father divided up his inheritance in verse 12, the object pronoun is plural: "He distributed to *them* his property". The older brother got his inheritance the same time the younger one did! His problem was, as time went on, he forgot that his faithfulness to his father didn't make him better than his unfaithful brother. He had not earned the inheritance—his father's grace apportioned it to him, as it did to his brother.

In a similar way, those of us who have been faithful to our heavenly Father for many years might forget he saved us by his grace through faith (Ephesians 2:8). Yes, we repented of sin and obeyed the gospel, and we have lived faithfully for decades in the house of God. But the minute we refuse to show God's love to those who struggle, we forget it was God's grace that has granted us a path to inheritance, the same time he gave them their portion of grace—at the death, burial, and resurrection of Jesus. They might have squandered their inheritance, yes. But even if they hadn't, Jesus still had to die because of my sin; we too needed the Father's forgiveness.

Luke shares a parable with us in Luke 7:41-42 to illustrate this principle: "Two men owed money to this creditor. One of them owed five hundred days' wages, and the other owed fifty. Since they did not have the means to repay, he forgave them both. Which of the two will love him more?"

He said this parable because a woman had entered the house wherein Jesus was dining, weeping and crying out to Jesus. While the attendees at the feast watched and criticized Jesus' seeming acceptance of her, she washed his feet with her tears and dried them with her hair. She continued to kiss his feet as she sobbed, to the disgust of the guests.

Simon the Pharisee, who was Jesus' host, answered, "I guess the one whom he forgave more."

Then Jesus gave several examples of the woman's love for him and compared them to Simon's oversights—he had not prepared a way for Jesus to wash his feet, he had not greeted him with the customary kiss, and he did not anoint his head to honor him as a guest. Jesus then notes in verse 47, "Because of this, I am telling you, her sins—many though they are—are forgiven because she loved me very much. But the one who is forgiven only a little loves only a little."

This tells us two things—one more apparent than the other.

The first is Jesus is merciful to forgive sin regardless of how bad it is. The second is what Simon needed to hear and what we need to hear today: If I do not love, I forget I was forgiven.

This outward attitude was present in the Hebrew Bible as well. Leviticus 19:18 is the passage quoted as the "royal law," which we explored in the previous chapter. But if you continue reading to Leviticus 19:34, he tells them, "You must consider the foreigner who lives with you as native born with you. You must love him as yourself because you were foreigners in the land of Egypt." The command for brotherly love was followed by a command for the love of strangers.

Paul reinforces this in Ephesians 4:32-5:2 (remember: the chapter break was not there originally!), "Be kind to one another and compassionate, forgiving each other as God forgave you in Christ. So be imitators of God like dearly loved children and conduct yourselves with love as Christ loved us and gave himself on our behalf as an offering and sacrifice to God for a sweet-smelling aroma."

To withhold our love for the lost is to forget we were once lost. To withhold our love is to forget God loved us first, before we did anything to love him. If you doubt at all what he meant by "supplement your brotherly kindness with love," use Paul's rule. It is not "the golden rule" (what we call Jesus' rule in Matthew 7:12, "Do to others what you want them to do to you") but the godly rule: "Do for others what Christ did for you."

## THE WORLD IS DIFFERENT IF WE LOVE LIKE GOD

> "I've always said I don't respect people who don't proselytize.
> I don't respect that at all. If you believe that there's a heaven
> and a hell, and people could be going to hell or not getting
> eternal life, and you think that it's not really worth telling
> them this because it would make it socially awkward—and
> atheists who think people shouldn't proselytize and who say
> just leave me alone and keep your religion to yourself—how
> much do you have to hate somebody to not proselytize? How
> much do you have to hate somebody to believe everlasting
> life is possible and not tell them that? I mean, if I believed
> beyond the shadow of a doubt that a truck was coming at
> you, and you didn't believe that truck was bearing down on
> you, there is a certain point where I tackle you. And this is
> more important than that."
> —Penn Jillette

This quote should make many of us Christians uncomfortable with what we let get in our way.

Penn Jillette is a magician who has been on radio and television for years as part of "Penn and Teller." These two magicians are atheists, and they speak openly about their skepticism of religion. After one of their shows, a man brought Penn a Bible and talked to him for a few seconds about why he thought it was important. That night, Jillette posted a video with the quoted statement on his website. He restated his atheism in the video and said that one person living their life right will not change that for him, but, "he cared enough about me to proselytize and give me a Bible."

As we start to examine where this last characteristic fits into Peter's list, an important question remains. Why would Peter use "brotherly love" in the same list as "love"? Should we make a distinction?

Since the structure of 1 Peter 1:5-7 is a *sorites*, brotherly love is a prerequisite for the capstone kind of love. Whereas brotherly love is directed toward fellow believers, the Christian's peak is found in loving everyone the way God does. We must "do good things for everyone, especially for those who belong to the household of faith" (Galatians 6:10). We must love everyone, especially those who are in God's family. In the same sense, we are to "keep ourselves in God's love" (Jude 21). "God proved his own love for us because Christ died for us while we were still sinners" (Romans 5:8).

God's love has a different effect for those who remain faithful to his family than it does for those who are outside, but he loves both. God's love for everyone led him to send his son into the world to save it (John 3:16). God's love for those who believe includes the forgiveness of sin. God's love for those who do not believe includes patience shown in the opportunity for them to repent, so they do not perish (2 Peter 3:9).

Our love for fellow Christians will be different from our love for others, but we must also love the rest of the world as God does, in that we will do whatever we can to save them. God-like love depends on all the characteristics from Peter's *sorites*. It cannot exist without them. As the capstone of the *sorites*, the overall structure is unstable if any supports are missing below, and those supports exist to hold love up in its place.

In Ephesians 4:15, Paul talks about the need to speak the truth (which requires knowledge of the truth) in love. James says in 2:15-16 that if we do not give our destitute brother or sister what they need (an act of love), faith does no good. John says in 1 John 3:17, "If someone has this world's goods, sees their brother in need, and shuts out his compassion for him, how could God's love abide in him?" Love does not exist without these other characteristics! As a storm can have hail, wind, and a cold front without being a tornado, one missing factor changes the whole equation.

Why is this important? Paul said in 1 Corinthians 13:1-3: "Even if I spoke in the languages of mankind and angels but did not have love, I would become a ringing gong or a crashing cymbal. And even if I had the gift of prophecy and knew all divine secrets and had complete understanding—or if I had enough faith to move mountains—I would be nothing if I did not have love. Even if I gave all I own to feed the poor and surrender my life so I could stand proud—it would do me no good if I do not have love."

Understand the extent Paul went to just to make his point. Without love, it does not matter whether you have special power given by the Holy Spirit. It does not matter how much you know. It does not matter how much faith you have. It does not matter how godly you are or how much you provide for your neighbor. John says in 1 John 4:8, "Whoever does not love does not know God, because God is love." Love is the x-factor, the password into the Holy Estate. Without love, our message is noise.

## IS THIS LOVE?

*"Love never fails."*
*—1 Corinthians 13:8*

The meaning of love in the New Testament is not difficult. Wait—it is not difficult to *know* the meaning. It is incredibly difficult to *do* what love requires! We referenced 1 Corinthians 13:1-3 earlier; now look at verses 4-8 to learn Paul's definition: "Love is patient. Love is kind. It is not jealous. Love does not behave recklessly—it is not arrogant. It does not misbehave. It is not self-seeking. It is not irritable and does not catalog wrongs. It does not rejoice at injustice—it rejoices with the truth. It puts up with everything, believes in everything, hopes in everything, and endures everything. Love never ends."

If you want to take a painful self-administered exam, substitute your name for each occurrence of the word love—"Josh is patient. Josh is kind." As you work through the list, recognize any characteristics from 2 Peter 1:5-7. Patience, kindness, self-control, faith, and virtue are all either mentioned explicitly or implied. Of course they are—love is the capstone!

Paul again describes love as a requirement in 1 Timothy 1:5-7: "The goal of our command is love—which comes from a pure heart, a good conscience, and a sincere faith. Because they missed these things, [the Ephesian Christians] have swerved into worthlessness. They want to be teachers of the law without understanding either what they are saying or the promises they are making."

The grammar here is easy to miss. In translation, we might misread this verse to say there are three goals of our command. Based on the noun endings of heart, conscience, and faith, however, all three are the object of the preposition *from*, which in turn modifies *love*. So the simplest form of the sentence is "Love is the goal of our command." This love comes from a pure heart, from a good conscience, and from a sincere faith. Again, love is the end result, and faith is the starting point. Everything should come from faith and aim for love.

Likewise, our love of God is wrapped up in our obedience to him. Jesus said succinctly, "If you love me, keep my commands" (John 14:15) and "You are my friends if you do what I command you" (John 15:14). When we act on our faith with a good conscience and a pure heart, the goal—the point of Christianity (love)—is possible.

When all the conditions are present, the funnel cloud begins to take its powerful form. It does not stay in the clouds of philosophy and debate—it sweeps down into a worldview disoriented by sin and turns it right side up again. And afterward, the world never will be the same.

If your faith is fruitless, it is without love. If it is without love, one or more of those supporting characteristics are missing. Look hard at yourself and determine where your weaknesses are. You will recognize them by their lack of fruit. You will see yourself at odds with the Father's wishes for reconciliation with those who are lost.

When you begin to supplement these faults in your faith, it will cause you to change. Your diligence and faith will drive you higher. Virtue, knowledge, self-control, and persistence will sharpen your faith like a knife, and you will bring God's will down to earth in godliness and kindness. Only then can you have the love that reaches down with the power of God to turn the world upside down.

# STARTING TO LIVE EMPOWERED (EMPATHIZE)

## PHASE 1: LOVE GOD

**See Him as the father with two lost sons.** As a child, I remember thinking the "lost" parables from Luke 15 were strange. First, if someone had one hundred sheep and lost one, that's not too bad! A 99% retention rate is pretty good, considering all the dangers a shepherd's flock might face. Could he not buy another one to replace the one he lost? What's the big deal? The same is true of the woman with ten coins. Could she not just get another one? I mean, it's one coin. (Cut me some slack here—I was a kid who thought these must have been quarters or some other relatively insignificant amount of money.) But when we get into the third parable, we cannot pretend it isn't a big deal. This father has lost a son. "I'll just get another one" is not an option. It doesn't feel the same. It doesn't cover the loss of the first one. And yet, it's infuriating how we will overlook the loss of a soul from our congregation by writing them off. "They were just seeking entertainment," or "We're probably better off with them gone." How do we think God feels about that? He is already bereft of one child, then here we are, spitting on the Father's forgiveness. Remember that two sparrows could be sold for a little money, and not one of them falls without the Father noticing (Matthew 10:29-31). When is the last time you thought of how much loss God has endured? Will you take the time to help him look while there is still time to save some of his lost children?

**Respond to your sins as the younger son did.** Only five verses are needed to tell the younger son's story of repentance. He sells his father's property, wastes the money, and starves in a distant country for some time. Now, figuratively speaking (this is a parable, after all), God has given us a deposit of considerable value—the gospel of his dear Son. When we become distracted by this world's concerns, we abandon him, just like the younger son did. All the wealth the father gave him was gone before he knew it, just as "all have sinned and run out of God's glory" (Romans 3:23). But the young man came to himself and took some humiliating and risky steps to reconcile with his father. He could have said, "I spent all that money; I can't go back until I've made some of it back." Instead, he recognized any humiliation he might endure is better than begging for scraps from the pig trough. How valuable is my pride? Should I let it cost my soul and the peace of mind I would get by reconciling with God? Think about how long the son must have had to travel from the "distant country," with no high-speed transportation. He had the persistence and self-control to keep going the right direction once he decided to return home. If you are dreading the "trip back," take inspiration from the younger son.

**Be ready like the father's hired servants.** I wonder if the young man's robe was clean and waiting for him to return? As the father spent his days scouring the horizon for his son, did any of his servants help him pass the time? These men did not have any rights to the property (remember, the younger son offered to be made a servant since he no longer had a claim to an inheritance). They spent every day doing the work they were hired to do—the work the son should have been helping them do. But when the father was ready to celebrate his son's return, they did what the father commanded. They brought the robe, the signet ring, and shoes for him. They prepared a feast in his honor and celebrated with the father because his victory was theirs. In the end, as the older son protested the celebration, they got to enjoy the fellowship and delicacies of the father. When we encounter lost souls who are trying to come home, let's learn from these servants and do as they did. After all, Jesus told the apostles, "When you have done everything you were commanded, you are to say, 'We are slaves with no value—we have done what we were obligated to do'" (Luke 17:10).

## PHASE 2: LOVE THOSE MADE IN HIS IMAGE

**Do for others what God did for you.** Go back again to the personal moral inventory you created for chapter three. Spend a considerable amount of time looking at your current failures. Then think back to how this inventory would have looked several years ago—perhaps before you became a Christian. How many disgusting faults did you have? How many times did you fail to do what the Bible said? How many times did you hurt God's family with ungodly attitudes? Now that you remember, think of the grace of God you received, allowing you to grow from what you were into what you are. What about the grace being extended to you now as you try to work out your current moral failures? Take that measure of grace and use it in your relationships with others. As God tolerated you, you must tolerate others. To become bitter or vindictive about someone's past faults, instead of trying to encourage and help them to improve, is to think nothing of God's love. You are being the older brother in the parable, telling your struggling brother that even though the Father forgives him, you do not. Do not deceive yourself into thinking you are being realistic or will not be fooled again by another apology—if you will not forgive, you will not be forgiven (Matthew 6:14-15).

**Stop keeping a catalog of wrongs.** In 1 Corinthians 13:5 one of the descriptions of love says it does not catalog wrongs. This can be a difficult habit to break. When you catch yourself at odds with someone—especially someone you love dearly—see if you find evidence of browsing your relationship history. "You always do this!" "Every time this happens, you ..." How would you know unless you are keeping track? Look at Luke 17:4: "Even if he sins against you seven times in one day and comes back to you seven times and says, 'I repent,' forgive him." Also in Matthew 18:21, when Peter asks Jesus how many times we must forgive our brother, Peter suggests seven times. This would be considered generous to the religious elite—their scribes taught three was the limit—but in verse 22 Jesus responds, "I am not telling you seven times but seventy times seven!" That will be quite hard to measure when you are not keeping count! But it's closer to Jesus' point—it does not matter how many times you forgive. If they repent, forgive!

**Loving God = Obeying God.** I bet the older brother resented his younger brother's defiance of their father's legacy. All those years, the older brother witnessed his father's grief and picked up the younger brother's slack in the daily workload. He said to his father, "I served you all these years and never once sidestepped your command" (Luke 15:29). First, however, he probably was not telling the whole truth. How many people can say honestly they never once disregarded something their parents told them to do? Second, I want us to recognize the dynamic in the relationship between them—the older brother was angry at the father because he was overlooking the younger brother's sins. Are you willing to stand face-to-face with God and argue that the fellow Christian you resented all these years does not deserve his grace? Does such behavior sound more like Jesus or the devil? If you think you know better about when to forgive than God does—my friend, you have deceived yourself. The prophet Jonah also fell into this trap, refusing to preach to Nineveh when God sent him. When he finally went in chapter three, and they repented at his preaching, he left the city angry because God changed his mind about punishing them (3:10-4:3). God asked him simply, "Are you right to be angry?" (4). Jonah spent the rest of the chapter arguing with God over whether he had the right to be angry. If you ask me, God should be the one to say when a person deserves forgiveness and tolerance. When we refuse to show it despite the commands in the New Testament to do so, we are the ones in need of forgiveness.

# –X–

# AFTERMATH

## A WORLD SET UPRIGHT

WITH THIS FINAL SEGMENT OF THE BOOK, I WANT to equip you with tools to create your own plan and follow your progress. This is only the starting point—you must apply diligence and your own faith when carrying out this plan, or it won't happen.

What you need to do now (if you haven't already) is begin using a planning system to help you determine what you value and what you are best equipped to do. Then figure out where you want to end up. What steps will you need to take? In what ways are you unequipped? How can you supplement those weaknesses?

We will take this one step at a time. If you have a planner that works for you, try to incorporate some of the techniques below into your current system. If not, other options on my website may help you. Whatever you choose, keep it simple and be consistent.

## MAKING (AND STICKING TO) THE PLAN

### START IN THE CLOUDS

A tornado begins to form several miles up in the atmosphere. Likewise, you need to begin by raising your perspective so you can look far into the distance. Use the following questionnaire to help you produce conditions favorable to your development.

1) Imagine one hundred years from now a biography is published about your life. The author dedicates a chapter to each characteristic covered in this book, and gives examples of how you excelled at them (one chapter on your diligence, another on your faith, etc.). What do you want this book to say about you for each chapter?

For this question, you need to be open-minded about your future potential. This is not the time for pessimism. Come up with at least one major lifetime accomplishment for each characteristic. If you want to get more from this exercise, note several life goals you want to accomplish. Some examples might be books you published or the number of people you helped with food drives. You might have lost a certain amount of weight or quit drinking and went more than three decades without another drink. You don't need to share this with anyone—it exists only to help you visualize success with all these characteristics. These goals must be specific, measurable, and attainable in your lifetime.

2) Why did these specific accomplishments come to your mind? What makes them important to you?

Sometimes you will struggle to remain persistent in reaching your goals. During those times, remember why you're trying to achieve them. If you want to be in better physical shape, why? It's easier to tell your body, "No cheating on the diet!" when you focus on your reason—you want to play more actively with your children. It's easier to make yourself exercise when you envision wearing those old favorites from your closet again. This keeps your goals relevant.

3) Review your list from step one and take a personal inventory. Where are you, and what areas need significant attention? What obstacles prevent you from being that person now?

Don't overthink lifetime planning. Treat it like using a GPS. Start with your destination. Plug in your current location to compare potential routes. Then determine which route is best. Step 1 was your destination. Step 3 is your current location. The next steps help you determine your route.

4) In the next five years, what items from Step 1 can you achieve? What improvements could you make in your personal inventory from Step 3?

Even if you don't expect to reach your goal for ten, thirty or fifty years, plan to make as much progress as possible in the next five. Practically speaking, if you expect to accomplish something in ten years, but you don't make progress for the first five, you are setting a five-year goal and procrastinating its start for five years. Instead, why not start now? You will never again have as much future as you do right now.

5a) Determine milestones for each of your five-year goals that you can reach in the next twelve months. What areas of special attention can you fix in one year?

Once you know what you want to do in the next five years, break those goals up into measurable milestones you can reach this year. For example, if your life goal includes raising your children to be faithful Christians, and they are young children, your goal will not be achievable for several more years; however, you can set milestones for this year that move you closer to the goal. For example, you might plan a nightly devotional with your family at home, discuss what they learned in their Bible classes, and (as Deuteronomy 6:6-9 says) talk about God and the Bible with your children throughout each day. I cannot measure how close they are to becoming Christians, but if I track what we do every day, I can determine whether we met our goal number of family devotionals this year.

# BRING IT DOWN TO THE GROUND

5b) Incorporate "have-to" events into your yearly plan.

Because we live in a real world with real people and real responsibilities, we need to account for time we cannot use as we wish. You probably cannot quit your job and still take care of your family, so your work schedule is an example. Holiday plans with family, birthdays, and other commitments also demand your time. These "have-to" responsibilities are to some degree unavoidable, but if you try to put your life goals into a schedule already filled with "have-to" events, you will quickly fall short, burn out, or both. If your commitments are too burdensome to let you make realistic progress on your life goals, it might be time to evaluate your commitments. Again, I am not saying you should quit your job, but this evaluation will cause you to cut some things you might have thought you couldn't. You might cut back on eating out and buying brand names to help you decrease overtime hours worked. You might limit what your children participate in at school to give family time a higher priority. If the "prior commitment" is harder to give up on than the life goal, you have a choice to make. Either the commitment or the goal is not as important as you thought.

6) Schedule your month with milestones and "have-tos" that will help you stay on track to meet your yearly goals. Decide which habits you need to develop in order to give proper attention to your moral deficiencies.

This is when your planning will start to feel intrusive to your routine. That is normal—and a good thing. It means you are changing your habits. I recommend tracking your habits a month at a time, since many can be adopted within 3-4 weeks. This doesn't mean all of them change each month—areas of need can continue to receive your focus for multiple months or even years. As you plan each month, take time to evaluate which of your habits have become second nature and can be replaced, and which ones continue to need your attention.

7) Schedule your week and day so you can meet your monthly goals.

Every week, you should review your monthly plan to check where you are in your progress. Consult your weekly plan each morning and determine what you can cross off the list that day.

8) Continue to evaluate your plan as you choose to say yes or no to other things that come up.

By creating your plan in this order, you have planned for your daily commitments and your life goals. These are the most important items on your planner. Anything else you have time to do is fine (as long as you don't overload yourself), but don't let new opportunities or commitments bump you off your plan. If it's a new "have-to" you forgot or did not know about when you planned your year, add it now and begin working around it. If you cannot meet a milestone because of it, choose which is more important. Otherwise, you are being driven by your circumstances instead of having an impact on them.

9) Stay in the clouds when you're in the clouds and on the ground when you're on the ground.

You will be tempted either to disregard your five-year goals or to overthink them. I believe this is the reason so many of us struggle with long-term planning. We either get distracted and abandon our goals, or we spend so much time looking down from the cloud level, we never make any progress on the ground. For each step you take in this process, look mostly at the step you're on and the one above it. For example, when you are doing your monthly plan (Step 6), spend most of your time looking at the current month you are scheduling and the current year (Step 5). You might glance at next month to stay conscious of your "have-tos," but other than that, stay in the month you are planning. Do not give much thought to your weeks (yet) or to your long-term goals. Once you step down from the cloud level (Steps 1-5a), you should stay out of the clouds until the next year. Your "have-tos" will need to be kept up-to-date, but they can be added quickly as they are scheduled.

The same goes for weekly and daily planning. When you plan for the week, be concerned only with the current week and the current month. As with the month, you might glance at next week for any approaching "have-tos" but only briefly. When you plan for today, keep your mind only on your weekly plan and what you want to do today. Remember Jesus' warning—"Do not worry about tomorrow because tomorrow will worry about itself—today is full enough with its own concerns" (Matthew 6:34). Stay with today!

## MEASURING (AND EVALUATING) THE PROGRESS

At the end of each year, you will spend more time on your plan at the cloud level. Do not focus on ground-level things here (Steps 6-9). Get back into the mindset of seeing possibilities and dreaming about where you want to be many years from now. The rest will come later!

1) When you think about your future biography, do you want to add anything new to the chapters? Are there any life goals you didn't mention last year, or can you perhaps aim higher on one of your current life goals than you thought last year?

2) Did you achieve any of your five-year goals? Celebrate!

3) Can you complete any of your life goals in the next five years?

4) Perform another personal moral inventory (as in Step 3). What progress did you make on yourself in the past 12 months? Is that acceptable, or is more work needed?

5) Review your annual milestones and evaluate where you've landed. Did you meet them, exceed them, or fall short? Can you still meet your goals on time,

or does your deadline need to change? What new milestones must you meet to achieve your five-year goals?

6) Continue to "Bring It Down to the Ground."

## FINAL THOUGHTS

Now that we have finished studying Peter's list of Christian characteristics, what happens next?

I hope you've seen throughout this study that these are practical characteristics, and we have no excuse not to employ them in everything we do. However, they are difficult to maintain. To have enough of one characteristic to supplement another requires a tremendous amount of personal development. Reading one book will not resolve that. Periodically, you might need to revisit parts of this book as a reminder, but your success lies within your ability to do these things consistently. Once you gain mastery over a small part of your life, do it again over another. At what point are you virtuous or godly by definition? That's hard to say, but if you compare yourself to where you were just a few months ago, you will recognize proof of growth—fruit.

If you put in the work to make these characteristics part of your lifestyle, you will develop a powerful faith that will be undeniable. You will turn worldliness on its head and demonstrate the power of the gospel to a world in desperate need of it. You will have purpose—to worship and serve God the way he commanded. You will maintain integrity, understanding, and strength in difficult times. You will remain when others fall by the wayside. You will bring God's will into action in the world around you. You will rain kindness on all, and the world will know without doubt you belong to Christ because you love as he did. Your faith will be undeniable and unstoppable.

All it takes for your faith to be unproductive is the absence of just one of these things. Observe Christians in the world—too many of them fall short in one or more characteristics, and their lack of effect on the world shows it plainly. Rather than putting the power of godliness to work, they are driven by their circumstances where they don't want to go.

They say they have faith, but it doesn't work. *Does yours?*

CPSIA information can be obtained
at www.ICGtesting.com
Printed in the USA
LVHW052210091120
671185LV00015B/2305